DESIGN{H}ERS

First published and distributed by
viction:workshop ltd.

viction:ary™

viction:workshop ltd.
Unit C, 7/F, Seabright Plaza, 9-23 Shell Street,
North Point, Hong Kong
Url: www.victionary.com   Email: we@victionary.com
 @victionworkshop
🐦 @victionary_
📷 @victionworkshop

Edited and produced by viction:ary
Book design by viction:workshop ltd.
Concepts and art direction by Victor Cheung
Cover story interviews and outlines by Lisa Hassell

Special shout-outs to the women behind this book:
Sauman Wong, YuetLin Lim, Katherine Wong, Leanne Lee
♥

ISBN 978-988-79033-2-1
Printed and bound in China

CON →TENT
DESIGN{H }ERS

4 STOR

S + 27 SHOWCASES

When I started writing the foreword for this book, I focused my attention on its name. For me, it immediately called to mind the term 'HERstory', a word coined to describe history viewed from a female or specifically feminist perspective, which is much of history outside the conventional narrative we all grew up with.

Upon looking back, I came to the sudden realisation that I, shamefully, could not name a single female graphic designer of note working before the 1990s. Where were they? Were women in the past discouraged to pursue graphic design as a career path or prevented from further advancement by a male-dominated industry? Were their stories simply lost to HIStory? The answer is a complex blend of many factors, but it was discouraging that I could not recall learning about the female equivalent of a Paul Rand or Herb Lubalin in any of my graphic design history classes.

The names of those who made their mark in the 20th century — April Greiman, Muriel Cooper, Cipe Pineles, Ruth Ansel, and more — only began to ring a bell after some internet sleuthing. As compared to the contemporary rise of female designers or the ones working today whom I am able to name without a second thought, it seems as though women are ultimately just beginning to make their way into mainstream graphic design history and awareness.

The reason why this book is truly 'A Celebration of Women in Design Today' is because we have so much to celebrate in 2019. We have come a long way in the past two decades alone. I know this, because I have witnessed the changes first-hand. The stars certainly aligned for me when I started my design agency, RoAnd-Co, in 2006, when businesses were becoming more interested in working directly with female designers. I met a lot of clients

FOREWORD
by ROANNE ADAMS

who were looking for that 'feminine sensibility', and I can see why! Women are inherently creative and inherently powerful. We all have spectacularly unique innovative powers under the surface, waiting to be unleashed, and it is about time that businesses tapped into those powers.

Regardless, we still have a long way to go when it comes to representation. It is unbelievable that only 12% of creative directors in our industry are female. As one of them (albeit self-appointed!), I feel a duty to help raise other female designers up. Women who are in positions like mine need to help other women unleash their potential and feel empowered to do what they feel they are intrinsically meant to do and create. Over the years, I have employed and mentored a great deal of exceptionally talented women, and worked with scores of female-led businesses. I love working with women because I get to witness their genius first-hand, and feel like I am actually moving the needle towards progress, equality, and effecting change.

I am honoured to have the opportunity to do just that, along with the other incredibly talented women in this book. Being celebrated within this group is incredibly flattering, and carries with it an enormous sense of pride. Pride that as so-called 'notable female designers', we stand out in the sea of male designers not just because of our gender, but also because of the inarguable quality and beauty of our work. Whether they are DESIGN(H)ERS whom I have worked with, those I have had the honour of speaking at conferences with, or ones I have admired from afar, they all have their own unique style and bring a fresh perspective to the design world with grace, flair, and finesse!

The future for women in design holds SO much potential. I imagine a world, another two decades from now, when 50% of creative directors are women and can say with certainty that our world will be a more harmonious place when that happens! Women can now disrupt status quo through our design and our leadership, and that is exactly what the women in this book are already doing. Now, the time has come: our time to create great work and most importantly, our time to make DESIGN(H)ERSTORY!

DESIGN{H}ERS

KEEPING IT REAL ↘ As was the case with many other professions in the past, influential positions in the design world were traditionally dominated by men, but times they are luckily a-changing. Diversity is slowly but surely permeating the creative industry, where classifications delineating sex, age, religion, and race are no longer beginning to matter as much when it comes to producing and recognising authentic, beautiful, and meaningful work.

To that end, women designers are freer to express themselves today; thanks to more open minds, open doors, and open refusals to be oppressed. More of them are basking in the successes of their efforts and the endeavours of those before them: a justified feat that comes at the end of a bittersweet journey fraught with bumps and battles fought together as a bad*ass team. While the future seems to lead down paths of infinite possibilities, there is still a long way to go before everyone else catches up to the fact that one's gender need not be a privilege or an excuse.

Throughout this book, four creative luminaries tell it like it is by sharing their personal journeys, observations, and advice for the next generation in Real Talk. By taking no bullsh*t and facing their challenges head-on, these women prove that passion, perseverance, self-evolution, and fearlessness are among what it takes to build rewarding careers against all odds, stereotypes, outdated perceptions, and prejudices – no matter where one may be.

REAL TALK #1
PURPOSE+ PASSION = POWER ↘

Jessica Walsh

Jessica Walsh

Partner, Sagmeister & Walsh

As a key figure at one of the most renowned agencies in the creative industry, graphic designer and art director Jessica Walsh is a force to be reckoned with. Although her work has won many major design awards and earned her recognition as one of Forbes's 30 Under 30, she shows no signs of slowing down yet with an ever-growing list of famous clients. In addition to speaking at local and international conferences, she inspires the next generation of designers on a regular basis as a teacher at The School of Visual Arts in New York. In 2016, she launched the Ladies, Wine & Design initiative, which has since spread to chapters in over 200 cities across the world.

Photo: Dusdin Condren

DESIGN{H}ERS

The bottle label reads:

NCF

My friends are poppin' babies but I'm poppin' champagne

↖ **Sorry I have No Filter**
Conceptualisation, art direction, photography, and product design for a Ladies, Wine & Design campaign that supports women in creativity and design leadership roles.

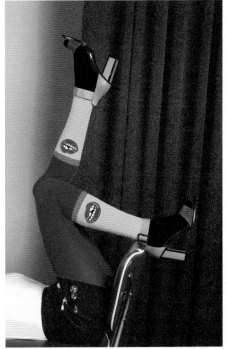

DESIGN{H}ERS

For an influential creative who carved her niche at a relatively young age, it comes as no surprise that success was not a walk in the park for Jessica Walsh. Armed with a penchant for hard work, a healthy dose of reckless optimism, and a whole lot of talent, she ditched the safe career path straight after school to pursue her dreams, a colourful journey that has taken her all the way to the top of one of the best design studios in New York City and the industry at large – Sagmeister & Walsh – where she has been one-half of the partnership since the age of 25. Her bold visual style and distinct persona seem to be a manifestation of her tenacity and artistic ingenuity, which she carries across all aspects of her work.

"Everyday is something new," she divulges. "Sometimes, I am on a photoshoot or a commercial set; sometimes, I am travelling to meet with clients; sometimes, I am travelling to give a lecture; sometimes, I am in the office in NYC working with our creative team." Having to flex her skills across creative direction, new business generation, client management, production oversight, and studio operations throughout the week, she values the contributions of her colleagues and the sense of camaraderie – staying connected remotely via Slack or other project management tools when she has to. "I ideate a lot of our work; coming up with tonal or visual directions, copywriting, and concepts. That said, I have no ego about something being 'my idea', and warmly welcome when someone in the studio proposes something that I had not thought of, or comes up with something even better than what I was thinking of. I love collaboration and think that having a mix of talented people with diverse viewpoints, backgrounds, and styles strengthens our work."

Between herself and Stefan Sagmeister, the other half of the studio's namesake, they divide what they direct to ensure ownership and accountability – often asking each other for advice, opinions, or help with ideas along the way. Besides finding solutions for a wide range of client briefs that deal with anything from branding and strategy work, advertising campaigns, and social media content creation to photography, editorial as well as exhibition design, Jessica also relishes opportunities where they get to initiate their own projects. "I believe that design is an incredible tool that we can use to start dialogues, motivate change, tell stories, or for activism. We do not always have to use our skills as designers to sell things."

↓ Pins Won't Save the World
Pin design for a non-profit project where proceeds were donated to various organisations in the USA, such as Amnesty International.

Timothy Goodman, a fellow designer and illustrator whom she met during her stint at PRINT magazine, has been a long-time collaborator in her non-work-related adventures. It was a creative partnership that was cemented by the blurring of lines between love and friendship in their 2013 social experiment, 40 Days of Dating (http://fortydaysofdating.com). After an intense few years of output, fatigue set in and forced them into a hiatus of sorts, but she is looking forward to working together again soon. "We have started talking about collaborating on new ideas, and have thrown out lots. It is (just) a case of waiting on the right one (that) we are both extremely excited about. These projects take up so much of our time, energy, soul, and money, so we really have to be super sure before we commit to a new project."

One of their best-known projects together, 12 Kinds of Kindness (https://12kindsofkindness.com) was based on 12-step self-improvement programmes designed to change behaviours, and revolved around inculcating kindness and empathy. "One important lesson I learned from this project is that women are sometimes unsupportive and cruel towards one another, and do not want other women to succeed. Often, this is subconscious. I think one reason for this is that our chances of success are much slimmer than our male counterparts. 70% of (design) schools are women. Only 12% of creative directors or CEOs of creative companies are women."

DESIGN{H}ERS

"People are always negative towards workaholics...no one person is the same, and to say that everyone has to separate work from life and go for yoga or hiking or meditation during the weekends is bullsh*t."

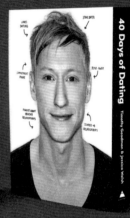

→ **40 Days of Dating**
Editorial design for a book featuring previously unseen material from the 40 Days of Dating experiment.

↑ **12 Kinds of Kindness**
A social experiment involving 12 steps to build kindness and empathy over 12 months, in collaboration with Timothy Goodman.

Inspired by her personal experiences that led to the 12-month experiment and its results, Jessica went on to create Ladies, Wine & Design (https://ladieswinedesign.com), a space where women could come together, help one another, and form more positive relationships with each other. "It started quite small and humbly, and I had no global ambition – that was never the intent! It was more like a rough idea (to) get women together and talk about interesting topics such as business, life, and money. A few weeks after the launch, I started receiving emails from women all around the world (who were) interested in starting their own chapter in their own cities. So, we set up the website and it just took off! This is a global grassroots project led by numerous talented, bad-*ss ladies who are championing, mentoring, and supporting women in their own individual cities. A lot of the other cities are running conferences or planning large events, and it is incredibly inspiring to see what happens when women get together," she enthuses.

More driven than ever to explore new ideas, Jessica seems to work more than most people and brushes the notion of busy weekends, evenings, and vacations away as something that simply comes with the territory. Unsurprisingly, that is just how she likes it. "People are always negative towards workaholics and there is so much mandate these days about how you have to 'find your work-life balance'. I think for people who do not find joy or fulfilment in their work, it is great to make that separation, but no one person is the same, and to say that everyone has to separate work from life and go for yoga or hiking or meditation during the weekends is bullsh*t," she observes. "I enter a meditative flow-state more easily while at work than I do on a yoga mat and find no appeal in going out every night drinking either. I find satisfaction and fulfilment from my work, and wake up each day motivated to build something I care about and believe in. I find joy in our work functioning for our clients' goals and touching their audiences; from people connecting to the work; from starting dialogues and conversations."

As devoted as she is to her job, Jessica enjoys meaningful moments outside the office: "I love spending time with my family and my sister playing cards or backgammon. I love trying new restaurants with my husband (and) going to the dog park with my dog. I love binge-watching Netflix (shows) and very occasionally, I go out dancing. I love to travel and am privileged that work has taken me to many places." She also commits a large portion of her time engaging with junior-level design students as a teacher at The School of Visual Arts. The experience has been eye-opening for her, as students benefit from a more professor-led approach and base their studies on industry-focused live projects to get a foot in the door to the creative industry. "It is a very different model than the (one at the) school I went to. Richard Wilde, who runs the graphic department, finds interesting working professors in the industry and provides no structure for how to run the course. Initially, I thought the lack of structure was crazy, but I have seen that it leads to interesting and worthwhile results."

For those curious about the wisdom she imparts in class, Jessica emphasises on the importance and value of building a solid portfolio for emerging designers to stand out. It is a foolproof lesson that she has applied to her own life: "I knew that with good work in my portfolio, I would be able to get more good work, and eventually, get great work that would also pay well. This strategy did pay off. Building a strong portfolio from working somewhere highly creative can pay off later on. If you are lucky enough to land a spot at your dream studio or agency, work your *ss off, and give it everything you have. Once you have worked there (for) a couple years, built up an excellent portfolio, and feel like you have learned everything there is to learn, it is probably time to move on – unless you can find new ways to grow."

She also believes in taking charge of the situation if the ultimate job is out of reach. "Create your own passion projects; become your own client. You have to be able to prove your talents and skills through your work before you can expect to get hired to create great work. If you put in the time and hard work in the beginning, it will pay off creatively and financially in the long term," she advises.

Having only had a few women to look up to in the industry during her college years, these days, Jessica is proud to witness many of her contemporaries doing well. "Most of my favourite creatives are other women. There is now increased awareness and intolerance of sexism; and more women idols and mentors than ever," she says. Due to the increased freedom that comes with the shift away from working in-house to more flexible freelancing arrangements, she has also been seeing more successful women in design, with

↑ MILLY
Conceptualisation, art direction, and photography for MILLY by Michelle Smith's rebranding campaign. Retouching: Daniel Plateado

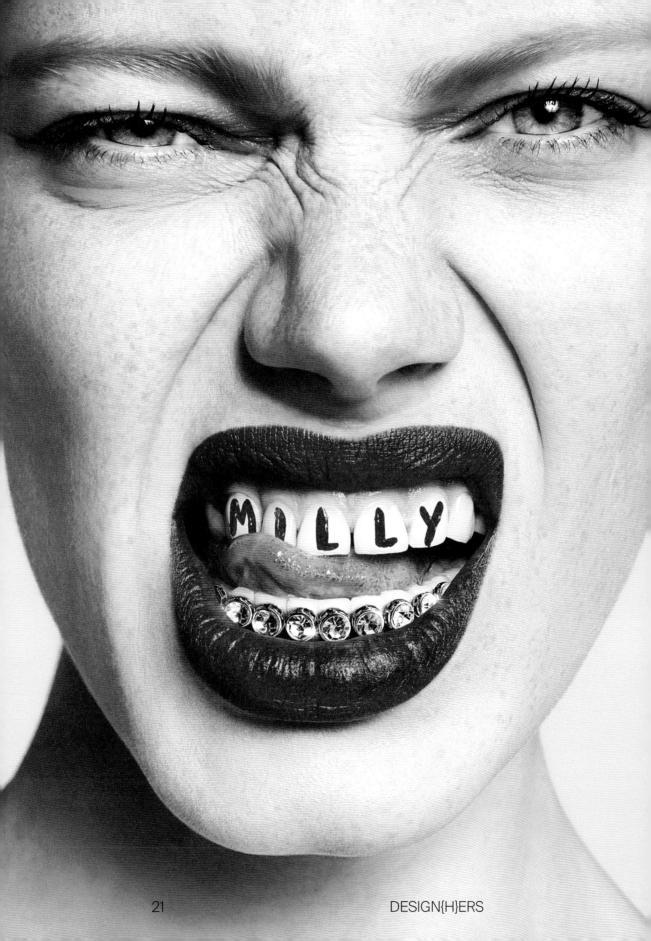

↳ MILLY
Conceptualisation, art direction, and photography for
MILLY by Michelle Smith's rebranding campaign.
Retouching: Daniel Plateado

some outdated barriers being broken down. "Freelance opportunities have exploded with the web and social media and I believe that this, combined with cheaper tools allowing for a lower barrier to entry, has helped democratise who can become a designer or receive success, work, and recognition. It is much better than it was a few decades ago, (because) it is less about who you are, where you are from, and who you are connected with; although privilege, gender, ethnicity, and background still can impact this."

Over the years, Jessica has weathered many storms of scrutiny and criticism, but she does not let negativity drag her down. Instead, her sights are set firmly onwards and upwards. "Haters are gonna hate. It is their right to have an opinion and not like my work. I appreciate comments when (they are) constructive criticism; if it makes me think and I can learn from it. When it is focused purely on hate or trying to tear me down, I just feel bad for these people. Who spends their time online trying to bring other people down? Only people who are jealous or dislike their own lives or circumstances, or are seeking attention. Now, I just try to avoid even looking for the negative comments or hateful tweets. I focus on my own work and putting things in the world that I believe in and encourage others to do this as well. I am really proud of the work we are doing here at Sagmeister & Walsh. I am proud we can create the work we do — which is highly creative, often not for profit, often championing important causes, and starting dialogues. I would not change a thing." Hater or not, it would be the world's loss if she did.

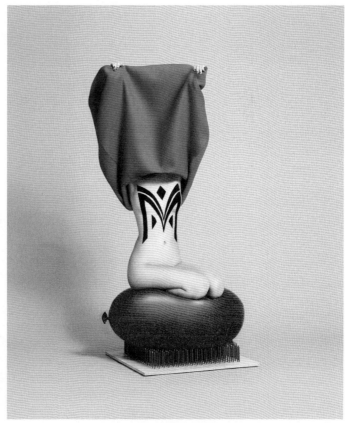

Carolina Cantante & Catarina Carreiras

"Sensibility is taking over practicality, and women are the perfect players."

Founded by Carolina Cantante and Catarina Carreiras in 2011, Studio AH—HA is a graphic design and communication studio that pursues a variety of creative interests across different mediums through brand strategy, visual identities, advertising, new media, photography, product design, and illustration work. With an ever-changing cast of collaborators, they take a holistic approach in turning their clients' inspirations, ideas, and motivations into fresh, engaging, and compelling messages that matter.

Visual identity and design development for Biocol Labs, a healthcare company focusing on chemical-free medicine. Photos: Diogo Alves

↑ Social Help
Visual identity and design development for Social Help,
a production company with a social take on special projects.
Photos: Diogo Alves

CAROLINA CANTANTE & CATARINA CARREIRAS @ STUDIO AH—HA   28

Q: What would you like to achieve through your work?

A: Simplicity, timelessness, and engagement.

Q: Where do you see the future of women in design?

A: We see a wider space for action, growing trust, and stronger voices; not just as a reflection of the times we are living in, but also in the pursuit of more sensible, deeper answers in graphic design. Sensibility is taking over practicality, and women are the perfect players – the ones who know and master the different ways to simplify and translate the dichotomy of today's world in an array of different environments and businesses.

Q: How can one become more creative?

A: Find the right time, space, and scale to let ideas flow. Sometimes, unexpected parts of the day can trigger free headspace – especially when you are managing a family at the same time. It is okay to live on a smaller scale to create greater bodies of work as well. What was considered dogma years ago is no longer true, and it is okay to live outside that spectrum.

We also believe in the importance of building a wide visual database of amazing, whimsical work that has nothing to do with graphic design, so that we can dig into it for the right puzzle pieces when solving a design need. Art, architecture, cinema, and literature are more important to the creative process than what our fellow designers are doing.

Q: Who are the women who inspire you?

A: Nathalie du Pasquier, Ray Eames, Charlotte Perriand, Helena Almeida, Ellen Lupton, and Hella Jongerius.

Q: What do you love about being a woman?

A: The wide spectrum of subjects that we can focus on within the same minute. The freedom to work with controversial and contrasting shapes and subjects at the same time. The unique sensibility that we have for putting together different shapes, fonts, and images. The love for colour and texture.

Q: Name the proudest moment(s) of your life.

A: The year we became mothers for the first time and also won a Young Guns award by the ADC.

Q: What brings you joy?

A: Time spent with our kids. The thrill of a new project and all the possibilities ahead. When clients become faithful friends. Living with the sun and by the sea. Finding time for self-discovery and research.

→ I Cinque Granni
Visual identity and packaging design for I Cinque Granni, a coffee shop with Californian vibes in Livorno.
Photos: Francesca Renzi

DESIGN{H}ERS

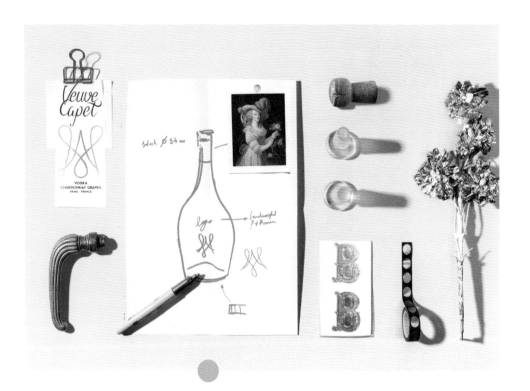

→ Veuve Capet

Visual identity and packaging design for a new chardonnay vodka inspired by Marie Antoinette, featuring a classic twist on the Dauphine de France's court spirit. Photos: Diogo Alves

CAROLINA CANTANTE & CATARINA CARREIRAS @ STUDIO AH—HA   30

→ Charlotte Juillard
Visual identity design for Charlotte Juillard, a French product
designer with a love for contrasts and colour. Photos: Diogo Alves

Creative director and visual artist Louise Mertens translates her admiration for purity, texture, materials, and the unique sophistication of Japanese art into visual concepts, creative/art direction, photography, editorial content, identity design, and artworks that are exhibited worldwide. Since setting up her own fine art studio in 2014, she has enjoyed entering into dialogues with images by employing manipulation in its purest form. She is constantly inspired by the human face and body, as well as all things mysterious.

📍 ANTWERP

Louise Mertens

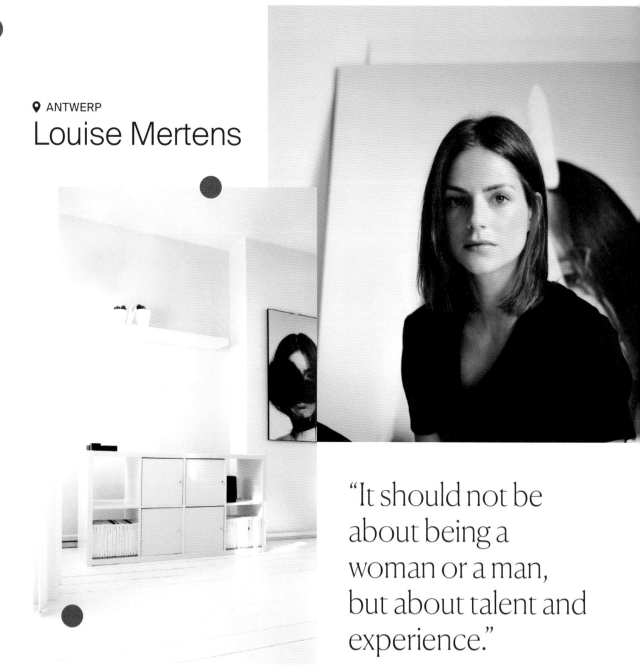

"It should not be about being a woman or a man, but about talent and experience."

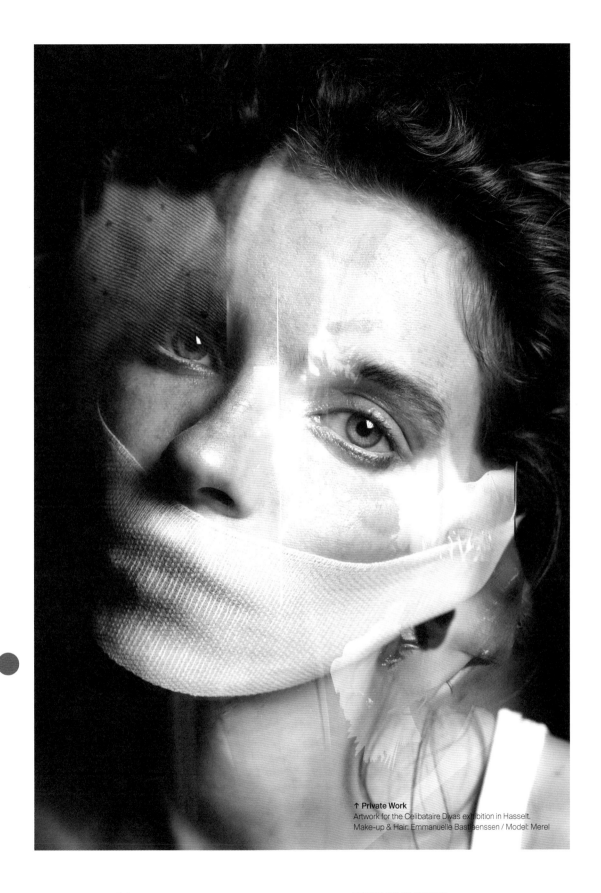

↑ **Private Work**
Artwork for the Celibataire Divas exhibition in Hasselt.
Make-up & Hair: Emmanuelle Bastiaenssen / Model: Merel

↙ **Fashion Special for De Morgen Magazine**
Art direction, visual conceptualisation, and artwork for the 2017
Fashion Special of De Morgen Magazine. Photography: Sophie
Coreynen / Styling: Lieve Gerrits / Make-up & Hair: Inge Devos /
Model: Lily Roberts

DESIGN{H}ERS

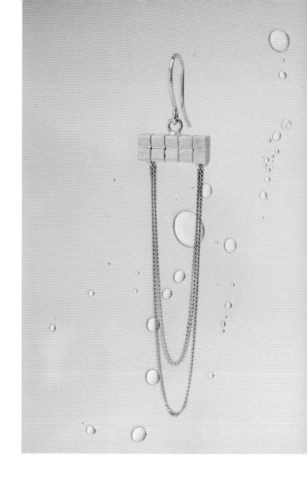
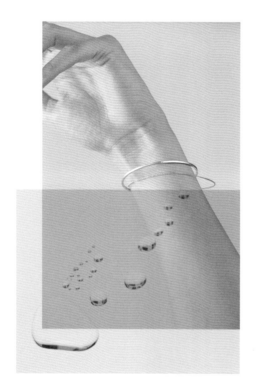
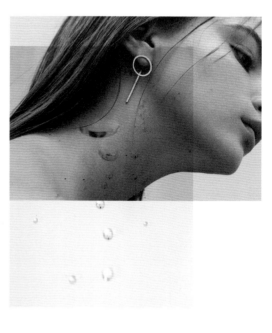

Q: What would you like to achieve through your work?

A: I learned that hoping for things to happen in the future only brings disappointment and stress. I try to live from day to day and enjoy little victories. My achievement is to be alive tomorrow and make beautiful things. Being able to stay grounded is an achievement to me.

Q: What will the future of women in design be like?

A: I love the movement that has been going on lately. Women are speaking up and it feels amazing to be taken seriously more often. I feel that it is my obligation to support this in any way I can, as a female entrepreneur. There is nothing more important than confidence and like men, women seek this in power, recognition, and being understood. I think what is important here is that it should not be about being a woman or a man, but about talent and experience.

Q: How can one become more creative?

A: Creativity comes in waves, always. There is no such thing as a super-human and we all need to charge our batteries once in a while. The biggest problem is that people often forget this part. The only thing they do is think about getting better, wanting more, doing more, overtaking the other, etc. Listen to your body and mind. Create time and space to just 'be' and let the inspiration come to you. Let go when you are stuck, be patient. It will come back before you know it. And when you feel a new creative wave coming, take it, and work like crazy. I live for this feeling.

Q: Who are the women who inspire you?

A: The women who inspire me are fearless and confident. They have an identity that is completely their own and an energy level that recharges me just by listening to them. I like women who are honest and real; who are not afraid to connect and not afraid of me. Women

that see beauty in other women that do great things, without envy. They are oh-so-hard to find but oh-so-precious. These are the women that I look up to and want to be surrounded by. Virtually or in real life.

Q: What do you love about being a woman?

A: I love this question as I always tell people how happy I am to be a girl. I refer to 'girl' as I still feel like one, learning so many things and still saying things like 'when I'm older, I will...'. I love having a soft voice, dressing up, and experimenting with fashion; making myself beautiful before going out, changing my hair, and feeling sexy in general. I'm not afraid to get my hands dirty but I love being elegant. I love my name. I can go on for days.

Q: Name the proudest moment(s) of your life

A: Going to Tokyo, Japan, at 17 for a few months all by myself. The day I officially started my own business in January 2014, I was so excited. My first solo exhibition and seeing my mother, sister, and grandparents proud. I will never forget their faces.

Q: What brings you joy?

A: My mother – what an amazing and strong mother I have. Everything she's been through and how much of a positive and happy person she is. Also, my partner – we've been together for 8.5 years and I'm lucky to have found a soulmate at a young age. The women mentioned above and my friends – giving me energy and support. Travelling – stepping out of my comfort zone and discovering that there's more than we can imagine. Standing still – thinking and talking about life, taking care of my body and being mindful.

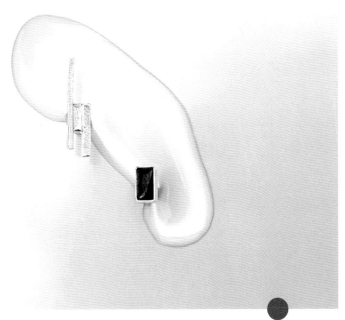

↖ **Jewellery Campaign for LORE VAN KEER**
Creative direction and visual conceptualisation using the shape of water for Lore Van Keer's handmade jewellery collection in 2017. Photography: Aaricia Varanda / Make-up & Hair: Emmanuelle Bastiaenssen / Model: Hannah T.

LOUISE MERTENS

38

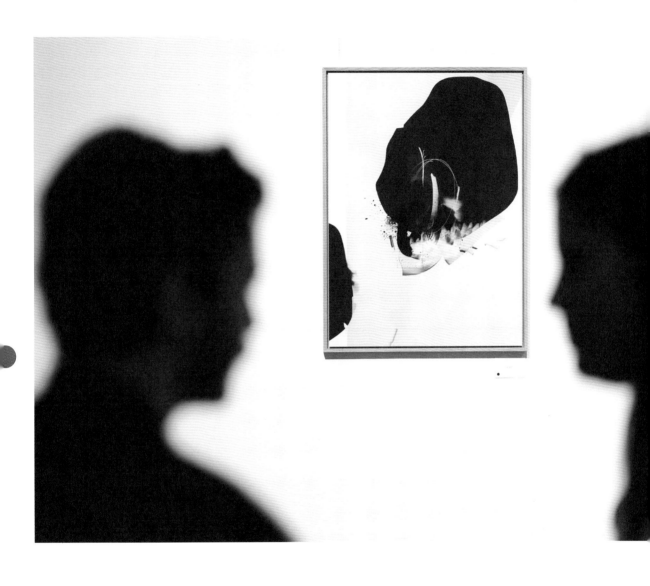

↑ **DEEP: An Artwork from the 'SEE' Series**
Artwork inspired by the Chasing Coral documentary in 2018 as part of 'SEE',
a self-initiated project capturing the beauty of the coral's dying process.

← **Book Cover for TIME OF THE TWINS by Kendall & Kylie Jenner**
Artwork and visual conceptualisation for a book by Regan Arts and sisters
Kendall and Kylie Jenner, featuring a futuristic collage.

DESIGN{H}ERS

📍 SEOUL / CFC

Charry Jeon

As the creative director at Content Form Context or CFC, a multidisciplinary design and photography studio in Seoul, Charry Jeon focuses on creating new value for businesses through thoughtful and effective brand experiences. She embodies the essence of CFC's successful design approach in the way that she understands and transforms content into relevant forms using the right contexts.

↘ **Vivevive**
Visual identity and packaging development for a period-proof underwear brand by Vieux et Nouveau (Blank Corp.).
Project Direction: Sangyin Lee / Styling: Studio Boucle / Lookbook Photos: Muted Studio

DESIGN{H}ERS

"I just want to design something that will inspire others continuously in the future."

↗ **Easy Peasy**
Visual identity and packaging development for an indie cosmetic
brand launched by Amore Pacific. Project Direction & Design
Implementation: Mamonde Design Team

Q: What would you like to achieve through your work?

A: CFC stands for 'Content Form Context', the approach that I personally pursue as a designer. It means always finding – and never losing – context for transforming content into a form. One of the most important aspects of branding is having a clear understanding of the brand. We, the studio team, then strive to find ways for this process to manifest itself. As such, brand design does not just end at a concept, but is constantly connected to a form. This is the way CFC designs, and we want to produce results that can be shared with the viewers.

Q: Where do you see the future of women in design?

A: In Korea, the percentage of female students in design schools is much higher than that of male students. However, about five to ten years after graduation, most of the designers out in the field and the heads of organisations are male. I think this happens in other cultures and societies as well, not just in Korea. Nevertheless, Korean female designers have been more active in recent years to improve their standings within the design field. Through these efforts, I hope that the era where women designers get more attention comes soon.

Q: How can one become more creative?

A: A phrase that I believe in is, 'you will see as much as you know'. The deeper you understand the brand you need to design for, the more parts will be revealed to you, so you can discover concepts you never knew. We analyse various data surrounding one brand from various angles and try to read patterns. We also get inspiration from artists and philosophers with novels or poems who share our concept of branding. Through this process, we come up with unique approaches.

Q: Who are the women who inspire you?

A: I have liked Paula Scher's typography-based work ever since my school days. Even now, at over 70 years of age, she is actively involved in a wide range of branding projects as a creative director, and this inspires me.

Q: What do you love about being a woman?

A: I don't think of any particular gender as being good or bad. I think that gender is just one of the many 'characteristics' given to an individual, much like race or nationality. That said, as a designer, I'm grateful to be a woman. Women form the main consumer base of many brands I'm in charge of, and for this reason, I can sometimes think of better solutions because we have an innate common understanding.

Q: Name the proudest moment(s) of your life. / What brings you joy?

A: I'm so glad that CFC, which was self-initiated, has now grown into a design studio with nine members. I'm also glad that more people resonate and are influenced by our work than ever before. This is why I feel responsible – I just want to design something that will inspire others continuously in the future.

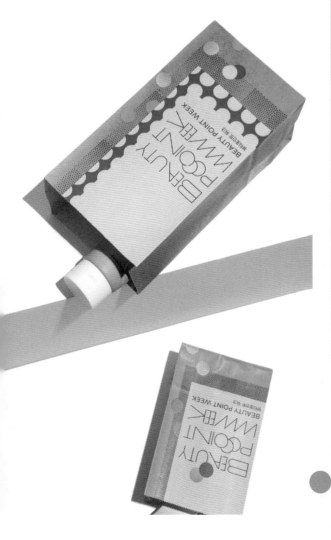

↙ Beauty Point Week
Visual identity development for a 2017 event that promoted
the accumulation of 'beauty points' through the purchase of
Amore Pacific-branded products. Project Direction & Design
Implementation: Amore Pacific Design Centre Retail Design Team

DESIGN{H}ERS

Founder and art director of Transwhite Studio, Yu Qiongjie, is all about pushing creative limits by dabbling in experimental styles through various mediums of communication such as art exhibitions, social events, and cross-industry collaborations – with comprehensive graphic design and visual branding being a primary focus. She is also a teacher at the Art Design College of Zhejiang Gongshang University, and a member of the Shenzhen Graphic Design Association.

📍 HANGZHOU / TRANSWHITE STUDIO

Yu Qiongjie

YU QIONGJIE @ TRANSWHITE STUDIO

46

↖ **2018 CALENDAR**
Design development for the studio as a self-initiated project.

DESIGN{H}ERS

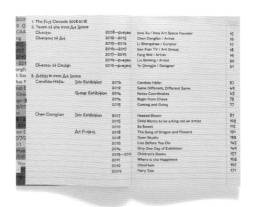

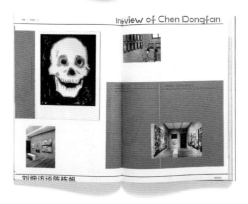

艺术家 Artists:
Bignia Wehrli
Candida Höfer
陈栋帆 Chen Dongfan
方伟 Fang Wei
Kiki Smith
廖文峰 Liao Wenfeng
Ushio Shinohara
Noriko Shinohara
Seton Smith
Walter Robinson
谢德庆 Tehching Hsieh
杨福东 Yang Fudong
易连 Yi Lian

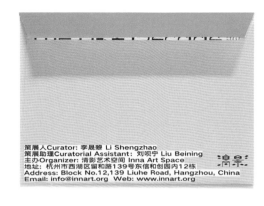

策展人Curator: 李晟嬰 Li Shengzhao
策展助理Curatorial Assistant: 刘呗宁 Liu Beining
主办Organizer: 清影艺术空间 Inna Art Space
地址: 杭州市西湖区留和路139号东信和创园内12栋
Address: Block No.12,139 Liuhe Road, Hangzhou, China
Email: info@innart.org Web: www.innart.org

← Inna Art Space 10
Design development for Inna Art
Space's tenth anniversary celebrations.

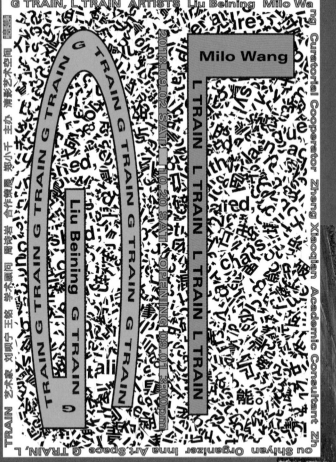

↙ G Train, L Train
Design development for a 2018 event at Inna Art Space.

Q: What would you like to achieve through your work?

A: In my opinion, communication is key – to communicate with clients to understand their intentions, and work with the design team to come up with better design strategies for projects.

Q: Where do you see the future of women in design?

A: Women are inherently more sensitive, emotional, and perceptive. I believe that these characteristics will be beneficial for female designers when working on design projects.

Q: How can one become more creative?

A: By experiencing life better.

Q: Who are the women who inspire you?

A: Dutch graphic designer Irma Boom and Japanese graphic designer Rikako Nagashima.

Q: What do you love about being a woman?

A: How value comes from scarcity.

Q: Name the proudest moment(s) of your life.

A: Being able to work on my interests while being a mother.

Q: What brings you joy?

A: Every time I create a design that I am satisfied with; when I see brilliant design work; when I buy a book I like; when I see a good exhibition; when I eat delicious food; when I travel.

FIGURES OF THE FUTURE
Design development for the 2018 International Creative Pattern
Design Competition in Hangzhou. Art Direction: XYZ Lab

AWATSUJI DESIGN

Founded in 1995, AWATSUJI design focuses on meeting its clients' requirements in every possible way by understanding their needs, collaborating for the best outcome, and challenging itself in the process to enhance its capabilities. The Harajuku-based graphic design studio believes that anything can be created using visual methods and hopes to fascinate audiences on the first impression.

→ **KINPU Japanese Gift-Money Envelopes**
Packaging design combining traditional binding
with a minimal modern pattern for Mark's Inc.

DESIGN{H}ERS

Q: **What would you like to achieve through your work?**

A: We are glad if what we design brings joy and smiles.

Q: **What will the future of women in design be like?**

A: (The ability to) expand designs without limit, and without being bound by being female.

Q: **How can one become more creative?**

A: Being interested in a variety of things and making good observations.

Q: **Who are the women who inspire you?**

A: Mother(s).

Q: **What do you love about being a woman?**

A: Respecting that we are women more than being aware that we are women.

Q: **Name the proudest moment(s) of your life.**

A: We like designing, and working with designs is part of our life.

Q: **What brings you joy?**

A: Having delicious food and encountering beautiful things.

↖ **Pleasure for Art: Junmai Sake**
Label design with graphic kabuki and geisha motifs for a commemorative sake produced in conjunction with the 2017 opening of the GINZA SIX shopping complex by Culture Convenience Club Co., Ltd. and Imayotsukasa Sake Brewery Co. Ltd.

→ Iinumahonke KINOENE

Packaging design in the form of a shopping bag and sake-flavoured castella or Japanese sponge cake boxes for Chiba-based sake brewery, Iinumahonke.

DESIGN{H}ERS

↑ Jiichiro Autumn Gift
Packaging design for an exclusive chestnut gift by
renowned Baumkuchen manufacturer, Jiichiro.

→ Takumi-Fu
Packaging design for coloured wheat gluten by
Kanazawa-based KAGAFU FUMURO-YA Co., Ltd.

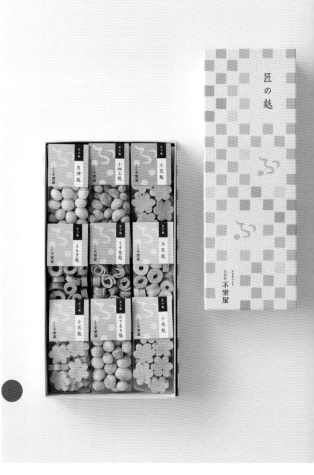

Eva Dijkstra

Eva Dijkstra is an interdisciplinary designer, artist, and co-founder of Sydney-based design studio, Design by Toko. Since graduating from the Academy of Fine Arts and Design in Breda, The Netherlands, she has worked with some of the world's best creative and corporate agencies across Europe, the USA, and Australia. Besides being recognised by various publications and having her work exhibited internationally due to her distinct creative approach, her innovative ideas and concepts have also been applied to a variety of local and global commercial projects.

⬂ East Sydney Early Learning Centre
Wayfinding system design based on children's building blocks
and the FF DIN Round typeface for the City of Sydney.

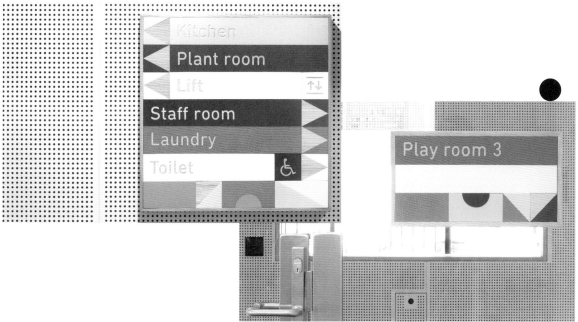

Q: What would you like to achieve through your work?

A: Joy and $.

Q: How can one become more creative?

A: Never look at other designers for inspiration. Instead, be as 'you' as you can be. This is where your creative joy and point of difference are most in sync.

Q: Who are the women who inspire you?

A: Carmen Herrera.

Q: What do you love about being a woman?

A: The freedom to be a bit of both. Wearing trousers one day, then a skirt the next.

Q: Name the proudest moment(s) of your life.

A: My daughter Pip, moving to Australia, and my first solo art exhibition soon after.

Q: What brings you joy?

A: Treading down unfamiliar paths, literally and meta-phorically.

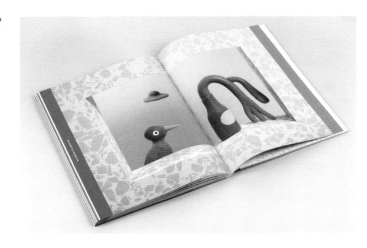

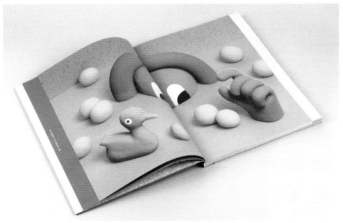

→ My Sister is a Martian
Editorial design for a book by 9-year-old Beau Neilson, where fantasy, facts, and fiction are intertwined.

DESIGN{H}ERS

↘ CULT 20 Years Anniversary
Design work for the 20th anniversary and exhibition of Cult
Furniture, featuring abstractions of the brand's iconic objects.

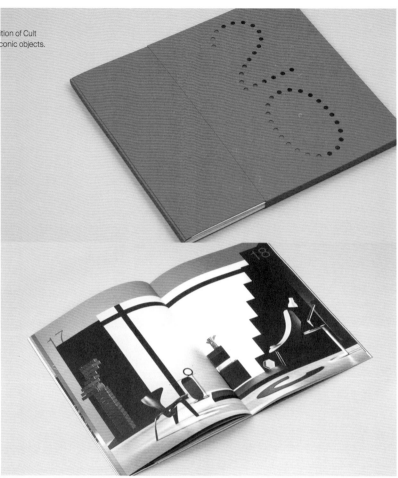

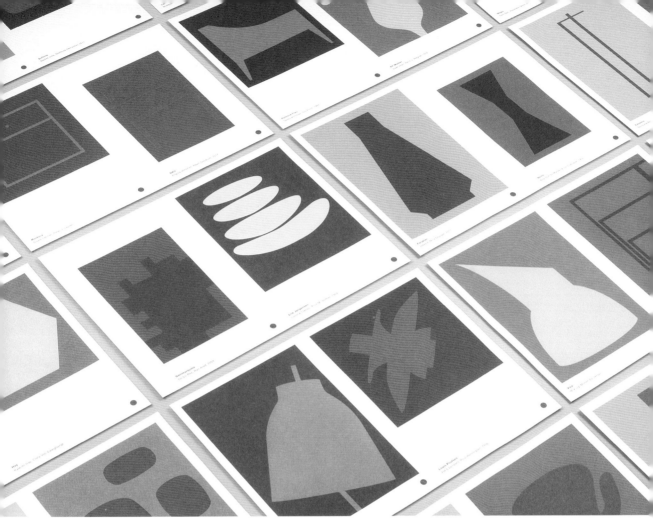

DESIGN{H}ERS

Susanna Nygren Barrett

"Life is too short to spend
on doing things that
don't make you happy."

Originally from Canada, Susanna Nygren Barrett is the creative director
and co-founder of Stockholm-based design firm, The Studio. In addition
to leading strategic design and branding assignments for both local and
international clients, she is a guest lecturer who holds workshops in various
design schools and has sat on numerous awards jury panels over the years.
Coming from a creative family, Susanna grew up passionate about music and
art, which continue to inspire her work to this day. She obtained her master's
degree from Yale University in Switzerland under the tutelage of graphic
design legend, Paul Rand, and renowned Swiss designer, Armin Hofmann.

↘ H&M Gift Cards
Card design to enhance fashion expression and maintain
timeless appeal for H&M's global audiences.
Illustrations: Aurore De La Morinerie. Case Photos: Patrik Lindell

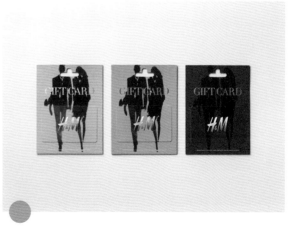

DESIGN{H}ERS

↖ Verso Skincare
Visual identity and packaging design for a premium skincare
brand featuring numerals to depict the reversal of ageing effects.
Photography: Damien de Blinkk / Case Photos: Patrik Lindell

Q: What would you like to achieve through your work?

A: For us at The Studio, simplicity has always played a key role in good design, not just as an idea in itself, but as the result of a sound design process. This requires relevance, restraint, and reduction; simplifying design and communication down to the essence. It allows a brand to stand out and be recognised in a crowded marketplace, while allowing us to understand as well as identify and hopefully, emotionally engage. There is also an aspect of sustainability in simplicity, in that good design holds up over time.

Q: Where do you see the future of women in design?

A: The best time to be a woman seems to be right now. As such, the future of women in design or any profession for that matter, we hope, is a bright one. Besides an increasing awareness of how branding involves tapping into both the rational and emotional values of a company and requiring insights from different perspectives, the buying power of women is also influencing the importance of how products and services appeal to them. At The Studio, we have a balanced team of men and women, and value the intersection of opposing forces – logic and intuition, reason and emotion – which reflects our manifesto: "Uniting art and commerce to craft brands with precision and purpose."

Q: How can one become more creative?

A: Although it may sound boring, we strive to find the solution within the problem itself. In Sweden, we say "dig where you stand", which to us means rather than complicate the problem, solve it by digging in and truly listening to the client. Design is a discipline with limitations, and it is what we do within these limitations that is the exciting part. Paul Rand once said in one of his lectures back in design school that "art is an idea that has found its perfect form", and this has always remained as some kind of hope for the design process; that the solution is there if you are just clever enough to discover it.

Q: Who are the women who inspire you?

A: Historically, the design profession has always included women within the decorative arts, textiles, ceramics, and crafts fields. However, there are surprisingly few female role models within graphic design, since perhaps they have not been given the recognition they deserve. This seems to be changing, and there are women artists and designers being celebrated now more than ever before. One example is the work of Margaret Calvert, who devoted a good part of her life to developing the English road signage and wayfinding systems while staying out of the spotlight. More names that come to mind as particular inspiration are the architect-designers Eileen Grey and Charlotte Perriand; photographers Louise Dahl-Wolfe, Lillian Bassman, and Lee Miller; along with talents such as Anni Albers, Ray Eames, and Lella Vignelli who worked alongside their partners. Currently, there is a fresh uprising of the female perspective within contemporary fashion photography, such as Annemarieke van Drimmelen, Zoe Ghertner, Lena C. Emery, and Viviane Sassen, inspiring a new generation. However, personally, the greatest inspiration for me would have to be my mother, with a creative force that persists even in her later years.

Q: What is the best thing about being a woman (when it comes to working with design)?

A: This is a sensitive question and hard to generalise, but I think women are naturally well-equipped to manage the design process. It is often a long, detailed process with many people and opinions involved, so building relationships and trust, as well as listening and having patience, maintaining a good sense of diplomacy, and multitasking are all skills that come naturally to many women. Being able to check your ego at the door and be a team player to work towards a common goal is important when working with a design team. And then, there is trusting your intuition. Female trait or not, I rely on this gut feeling daily.

Q: Name the proudest moment(s) of your life.

A: It is hard to isolate any one moment, but I think in the day-to-day design profession, the most satisfying moments come when the client is thrilled with the work. This confirmation that you have been able to interpret their needs and hit the mark is a great feeling. Of course, winning awards is nice and confirmation from our peers that we are doing well, but I think seeing the success of brands or products in the market due to good design truly confirms that we can make a difference. I am very proud of The Studio and to be able to work with our talented team of individuals everyday.

Q: What brings you joy?

A: Wow, this is quite a question! Perhaps it is having purpose? Knowing what I want to do with my life, and what to focus on. Being careful about my time; who I spend it with, and what I do with it. Focusing on quality in every aspect – from the person we choose to be with to the work we do, the type of clients we work with, and the people we surround ourselves with. Life is too short to spend on doing things that do not make you happy. Personally, I think that art or design schools offer a good exercise in getting to know oneself, and as painful as that process can be, I am grateful that questions like these came up very early on for me. You need to know who you are and what you want to be able to make these judgments everyday. This way of thinking is very important for having a direction, an opinion, a process, and a way of working with design. Fortunately, in Sweden, women have all the opportunities in the world to have both a family and a career, so perhaps, joy comes when all of these aspects come together in balance.

DESIGN{H}ERS

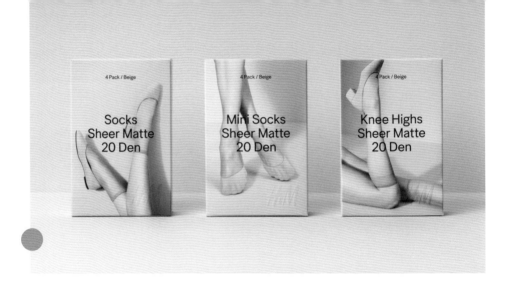

→ H&M Tights
Packaging design with a refined modern approach featuring black-and-white photography by Annamarieke van Drimmelen.
Case Photos: Patrik Lindell

Shaping
High Waist
Tights

30 DEN / SEMI SHINY

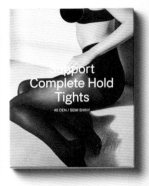

Support
Complete Hold
Tights

40 DEN / SEMI SHINY

Shaping
Cooling Effect
Shorts

80 DEN / SEMI SHINY

Bare Legs
Light Support
Tights

7 DEN / MATTE

Push Up
Bottom Lift
Tights

70 DEN / SEMI SHINY

Control Top
Tummy Hold
Tights

30 DEN / MATTE

↖ **Charitea**
Packaging design for a new series of classic dry teas.
Still Life Photos: Erik Lefvander / Product Photos: Patrik Lindell

DESIGN{H}ERS

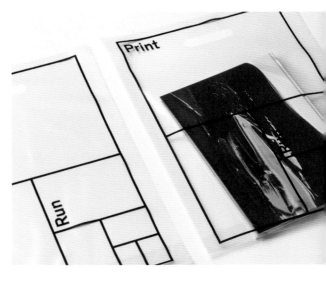

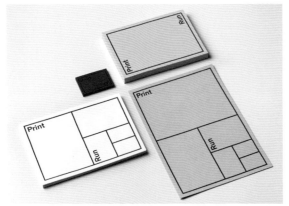

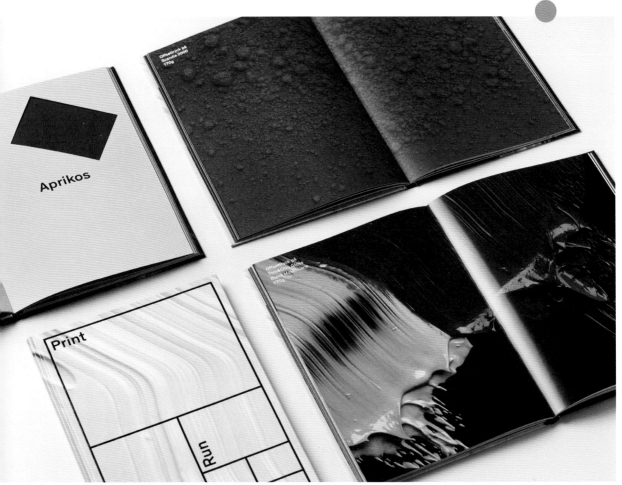

REAL TALK #2
FINDING POSITIVITY IN PERSISTENCE

↘

Verònica Fuerte

Verònica Fuerte

Founder, Hey

To have a place to call her own where she could explore her lifelong obsession with colour freely, graphic designer and illustrator Verònica Fuerte founded Hey in 2007 and has never looked back. Crediting their work with Monocle in 2012 as a pivotal moment in the studio's creative trajectory, their impressive client list has since grown to include the likes of Apple, Vodafone, The Wall Street Journal, Penguin Random House, and Oxfam, to name but a few. In 2018, they celebrated their tenth birthday by showcasing some of their best projects in 'Hey: Design & Illustration', a special-edition book published by Counter-Print. Describing her unique aesthetic and strong visual style as "geometric, colourful, direct, and fresh", she continues to hone her creativity and craft across a variety of mediums and fields.

DESIGN{H}ERS

Barcelona is a cultural hub that has teemed with creativity for centuries. Besides the lingering influences of traditional arts and crafts, the Catalan modernism movement also continues to inspire wonder through the indelible marks it left on the city's architectural landscape, whether it is via Antoní Gaudi's iconic masterpieces like the Sagrada Familia, or UNESCO World Heritage Listed sites like the Palau de la Música Catalana by Lluís Domènech i Montaner.

Over the last few decades, the city has evolved even further into a vibrant and thriving design hotspot, populated by independent labels, brands, and studios that position it firmly on the global map as an industry trailblazer.

Spearheading that scene today is Hey. With a catchy name that can be construed as a friendly greeting, a sense of optimism permeates their portfolio, which features the thoughtful use of bold geometry, clean typography, and a lively colour palette – an eye-catching style that is summed up by founder Verònica Fuerte as works that effectively "transform ideas into communicative graphics".

Founding it in 2007 after seven years spent earning her stripes at a variety of studios around Barcelona, Verònica has come to value the special kind of synergy that results from retaining a small studio size in order to achieve the distinctive and impactful outcomes that they are known for.

"We are a small team (and) tend to have one designer leading a project, but if the project is very big – which does not happen so often – we work collaboratively. As the studio director, I give creative art direction, but we always share ideas, and the best thing about being a small studio is that we all support each other. I like to keep it small because I think we have a very strong style, and if the studio grows, we (could) lose that style. When you are small, you have more control over that."

As a key figure in the studio, Verònica was involved in many aspects of managing it until she started a family, and striking the right balance between her work and home lives has become a new challenge. Accustomed to working late or odd hours in the early days, she has had to make some necessary adjustments as a business owner, creative, and mother to utilise her time more effectively.

"I think (that) when you are parent, the drive is stronger. Before (this), all my energy and efforts were focused on the studio and working. Now, I find that I am more effective during smaller blocks of time. I have been forced to prioritise, (but) it is positive because you manage your time better. It has not changed how I approach my work, or mean that there is less effort involved in my work. I just do not waste time anymore."

Mi *seño* voluntaria en el Centro es la mami de mi amigo Raúl. Por las tardes me dedica un ratito de su tiempo y juntas vamos creciendo y aprendiendo.

Carácter voluntario.

La creatividad al principio x Hey. Esta campaña nace como resultado de un fin de semana de talleres creativos planteados por el estudio de diseño gráfico Hey y coordinados por Cruz Roja Española. Los talleres se celebraron en el centro de atención a la infancia El Pinar de Loja, en Granada. Los niños y niñas, los voluntarios y el equipo de Hey trabajaron en la interpretación creativa y plástica de los siete Principios sobre los que versa y actúa Cruz Roja.

El Pinar
centro social
y de atención
a la infancia

✚ Cruz Roja

↓ **La Creatividad al Principio**
Poster design for a 2016 Red Cross campaign by Cruz Roja, using creative work produced by children at the El Pinar youth centre.

Pepa y yo pasamos mucho tiempo juntas, y me enseña muchas cosas nuevas... ¡Pero lo que más, más me gusta, son sus brazos calentitos y sus besos de gominola!

Humanidad.

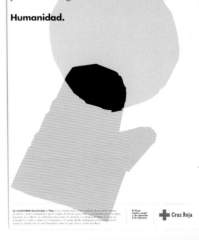

Con Carmen y Assita me río y juego. En Navidad cantamos Villancicos y en febrero decoramos todo el Centro con farolillos rojos y celebramos el Año Nuevo chino. ¡Y me encanta cuando leemos cuentos de *Las mil y una noches*!

Independencia.

En unos días nos mudamos a Barcelona. ¡Estoy muy nerviosa! Me he sentido muy cuidada aquí… Pero mi papi dice que no de preocuparme porque Cruz Roja seguirá sie nuestra familia.

Unidad.

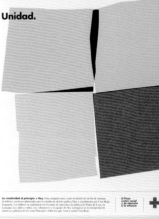

luntaria en el Centro es la mami de Raúl. Por las tardes me dedica un tiempo y juntas vamos creciendo do.

oluntario.

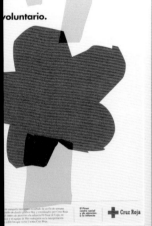

Por el Centro pasan muchas personas; niños y mayores. Y todas, ¡todas! son escuchadas. Da igual que pase el tiempo y haya cosas que cambien, ¡eso no cambia nunca!

Neutralidad.

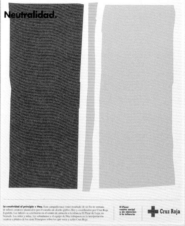

En el Centro jugamos muchas veces al ajedrez. ¡Y me flipa! Aprendemos a seguir las reglas del juego y al mismo tiempo nos divertimos. ¡Las reglas son iguales para todos, porque todos somos iguales!

Imparcialidad.

Rather than slow down completely, she has found clever ways to cope. To ensure maximum productivity, the studio has embraced the benefits of technology. Having been around for as long as they have with a diverse mix of clientele, they actively go online, particularly on Instagram, to win projects and engage with their audiences worldwide. "At the beginning, I made a lot of effort to get new clients by sending physical portfolios out over the years, but nowadays, clients often contact us through social media," she observes.

By widening their reach and sharing their aesthetics with a broader market, they have also been getting more exciting briefs, including the rare chance to develop new visual identities for one of the biggest co-working spaces in Barcelona, as well as a young organisation that raises money to run social projects – the latter being an opportunity that she values. "We try to work on a charity project every one to two years. It is important to give something back."

That said, social media has not been the studio's sole means of obtaining interesting connections. Represented internationally by Handsome Frank (www.handsomefrank.com), a UK-based illustration agency specialising in advertising and branding, they are kept very occupied. "We have to turn work down because we are a small studio and do not always have the capacity to take the projects on. It is a good relationship because they can reach clients that we cannot find (ourselves)."

Even though maintaining a modest team is important to her, Verònica clarifies that budget is not a main point of consideration when it comes to choosing what they work on, contributing to their assorted client list. "We do not discriminate at the beginning against any particular brand or company," she notes. What drives her instead is curiosity, which is why the pursuit of side projects is encouraged in the studio. Aware that client briefs do not always afford them the time to explore fresh ideas and techniques, she welcomes creative expressions on different canvases to inject new energy into their commercial work.

Recently, they began working with fabrics to increase their client base, and complementing their studio practice with an online store has fuelled experimentation, not only in their signature prints and posters, but also through bespoke fabric designs. Their first textile exhibition was held in 2017: "We made a scarf and a blanket, and it is really nice to move away from paper!"

From the outside, it may seem that their rise to early success was effortless, but Verònica reveals that sustaining the studio's momentum over the years has been, at times, challenging. "Many people think that it looks easy, like – oh, you are from Hey, and you do amazing things – but they do not see how much work is involved."

As proud as she is of everything that they have achieved, she also acknowledges that it takes hard work to consistently maintain energy levels and standards. However, she believes that finding the right designers who share the studio's philosophy and vision has been imperative since the beginning. "A studio takes a lot of effort; not only in designing, but also in investing in the people you work with, as well as the clients. Nobody teaches you how to run a studio or manage people. I made a lot of mistakes in the beginning, but you learn from them."

Although she has met many different people both locally and internationally throughout her career, she has been fortunate not to have faced much discrimination first-hand, and attributes this to cultural attitudes. "It has only happened to me twice in 11 years, (but) it is noticeable when it happens. I have been very lucky. Most of our clients come to us directly because they like the work, and they are not concerned with the people behind the work so much. In my experience, I think there are some clients and companies, particularly larger ones, that are more comfortable dealing with men."

While this might have played a part in how far Hey has come, establishing one's own design practice requires sacrifice and effort, and looking back, Verònica is reminded of how absolutely essential gaining experience by working for other studios was before she made the leap. "I was 27 when I founded the studio, so it was good that I had amassed knowledge from working in big companies and smaller studios. I do not think I could have done what I did without doing that first."

Underlining the virtues of patience and perseverance, she assures emerging designers that nobody expects them to have all the answers yet. "I definitely do not think that you are ever ready when you leave university! It takes years of work, internships, and trying different studios to find your way."

She also recognises how instrumental the right support is, knowing how tough it can be to start out without any connections in an industry that relies on a lot of relationships. Although she did not have many friends who had their own studios when she was starting out, her ex-partner at the time was a designer who really encouraged her to push forward. "My parents also gave me some good advice," she continues.

Advising graduates to seek any form of guidance as early as they can, she recommends reaching out to other studios and freelancers for tips, without letting ego get in the way of building a solid and reliable network. "I was afraid of asking for help when I first started out, so I would encourage anyone looking to start their own studio to get some advice in the beginning. Do not be afraid to admit that you do not know the answers."

Whether it is her determination and resourcefulness or her positivity that radiates all the way through her work, Verònica is living proof that persistence is its own reward.

↗ **FUGA Collection**
Design work for a self-initiated project-turned-textile exhibition in 2017, featuring the studio's first non-paper product.

DESIGN{H}ERS

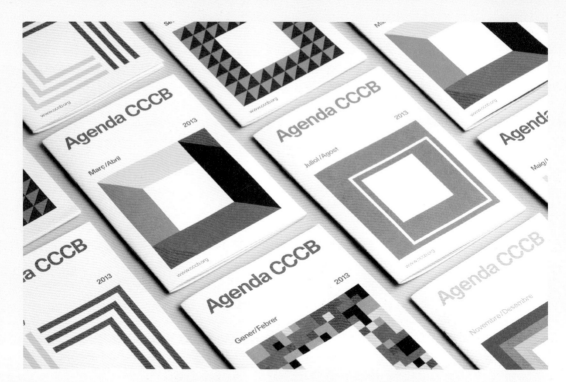

↖ **CCCB: Agenda CCCB**
Editorial design for the Centre de Cultura Contemporània de
Barcelona's bi-monthly printed programme in 2012 and 2013.

"I was afraid of asking for help when I first started out, so I would encourage anyone looking to start their own studio to get some advice in the beginning. Do not be afraid to admit that you do not know the answers."

↘ **CCCB: Agenda CCCB**
Editorial design for the Centre de Cultura Contemporània de Barcelona's bi-monthly printed programme in 2017.

DESIGN{H}ERS

→ CCCB: Kosmopolis
Visual identity and collateral design for the Centre de Cultura
Contemporània de Barcelona's biennial literature festival in 2017.

↑ **UNIQLO**
Packaging design in the form of shopping bags for the
launch of Japanese brand Uniqlo's first store in Barcelona.

Lotta Nieminen

Photo: Luca Venter

"I think finding your own voice is important, but I've tried not to treat it as something that can never change."

As the founder of a multidisciplinary studio creating holistic visual solutions for clients across disciplines, Finland native Lotta Nieminen is passionate about finding the best tools to execute content-driven visuals, working as a creative partner in bringing brands to life through thoughtfully crafted print and digital implementations. She set up her New York-based workspace in 2012 after studying graphic design and illustration at the University of Art and Design Helsinki and the Rhode Island School of Design. Besides being recognised as one of Forbes's 30 Under 30, an ADC Young Gun, and a New Visual Artist by Print magazine, she has also given talks at conferences and educational institutions in the USA and Europe.

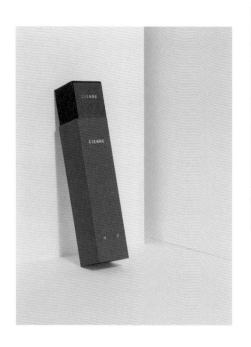

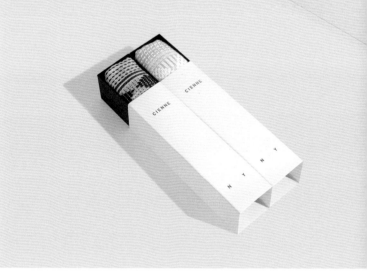

← CIENNE

Visual identity, print, and packaging design for Cienne, an environmentally and socially conscious ready-to-wear collection for women. Campaign Photos: Sarah Blais

DESIGN{H}ERS

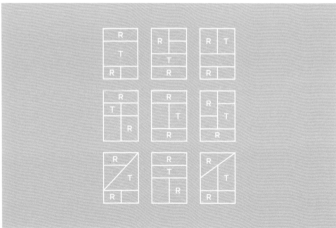

↗ Rent the Runway
Visual identity design for an online service that leases designer
dresses and accessories for a fraction of their retail price.
Campaign Photos: Marko Macpherson / Printed
Implementations: Renée Graham-Bastien

LOTTA NIEMINEN

DESIGN{H}ERS

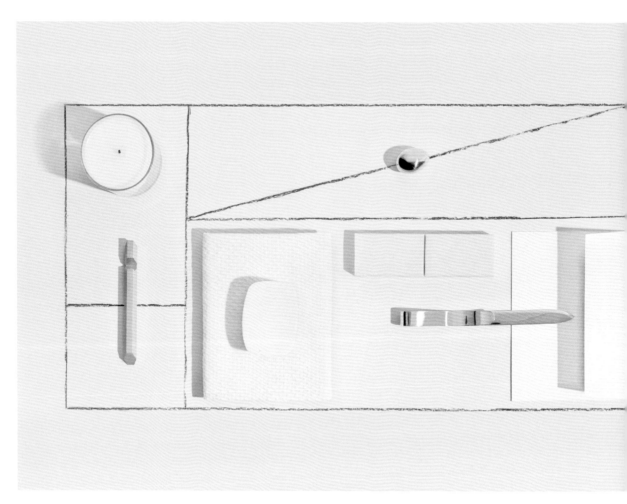

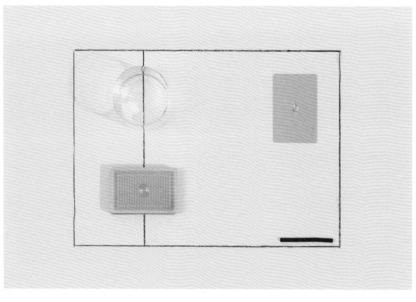

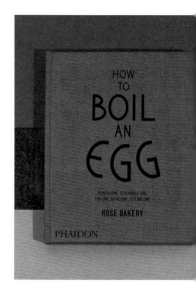

LOTTA NIEMINEN

94

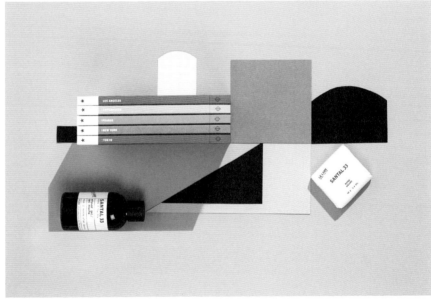

↖ The Line
Art direction and prop styling for The Line's 'Gifts to Delight the
Discerning' holiday guide in 2014, featuring purposeful gift ideas.
Photos: Hanna Tveite

DESIGN{H}ERS

Q: What would you like to achieve through your work?

A: Being driven and motivated is more important to me than having a very clear end result in mind. I feel like setting specific goals would close my eyes to opportunity, and that a lot of what's happened in my life wouldn't be the same if I'd had everything too planned out. Sometimes, I envy people who have very specific aspirations they strive towards: they seem so strategic and focused, but I'm happy with the natural way I progress, where my achievements build on one another.

I'm inspired by working in as multidisciplinary of a way as I can. Realising that I can identify as both a graphic designer and an illustrator was a big revelation for me at the time. When I started my graphic design studies, I built my professional identity heavily on being a designer: I thought that you should try to master one thing well, instead of hustling around doing a bunch of things with mediocrity. It wasn't until after my exchange semester at the Rhode Island School of Design that I decided to pursue illustration as an equal part of my professional practice. I realised that you can develop multiple visions and voices simultaneously – and not only is it doable, but the different type of work will also feed one another. Progress and development can actually lie in exploring things from another perspective: I think this applies to life in general just as much as work.

Nowadays, my professional identity is much looser: I find it important not to be stuck to one specific way of doing, and try to approach projects in as overarching of a way as possible by being part of multiple touchpoints in a project. For that reason, my current interest is in finding new ways to look at how the identities I create manifest themselves as interiors, or as moving images.

To me, a style is an ever-evolving process. I think finding your own voice is important, but I've tried not to treat it as something that can never change. I think the evolution happens by itself, out of a natural yearning for change and looking for new challenges. One reason designers and illustrators often end up sticking to one style is the fact that you mostly get commissioned and referenced on the work you've already done: the kind of work you have in your portfolio is the kind of work you'll get commissioned to do. Pushing past that can help in attracting new types of work. I've found that seeking new challenges by working with mediums that are new to me is often a good way to gain a new perspective towards the work.

Q: Where do you see the future of women in design?

A: While things seem to generally be moving in the right direction, women are still clearly under-represented in design. This can be seen very clearly at many conference line-ups, which still consist pretty heavily of (white) men. Filling a quota is important, because it stops organisers from being lazy: there's a ton of talented female-identifying designers, but it can take more work to find them, since they're still outnumbered by men in visibility. Luckily, there are some great resources online to expand beyond the usual suspects, such as Women Who Draw, Ladies, Wine & Design, and People Of Craft, to name a few.

As long as it feels necessary to highlight a designer's gender, it's obvious we're not where we should be. I'm pretty sure none of my female peers wants to be a good female designer – just a good designer would be great! Men rarely get asked how it feels to be a man in the design industry.

It is also extremely important to have this conversation be intersectional – it is not just about lifting up women, but all minorities. Yes, the design industry is gendered, but it is also very much racially unbalanced, not the least because of the political climate. I think in the past years, there've been strides for more inclusiveness – there's so much work to be done – but I think the discussion is a start. Equal representation is in everyone's benefit, and giving room and platforms to people in the industry who have a harder access to it is a duty for all designers.

Q: How can one become more creative?

A: I've found that stepping away from your desk is by far the best way to get new ideas and perspectives to the work you do. We contain many facets in addition to our professional one, and I think it's important to feed them all. To me, sitting at a computer is not the place to get inspired – it's where you put the inspiration to work. Therefore, not seeking any experiences outside of the desk can quickly result in a terrible creative block. I try to schedule enough things outside the studio: meeting friends, going to the movies or an exhibition, reading a good book... To me, these experiences and emotions are important things that feed the thinking behind the work – more so than straightforward visual inspiration.

To me, creativity is about not being too confined to a title or role you're given, or have given yourself. It is important to stay curious and flexible: ultimately, creativity is about finding the best way to manifest an idea.

Q: Who are the women who inspire you?

A: My mom, who is a fine artist and from whom I've gotten a love for colour. When we were little, she would stop me and my sisters to look if she'd spotted a "gorgeous shade of green". Once you learn to look for them, you start seeing inspiring colours everywhere! I always try to take snapshots if I see a beautiful colour combination, to later integrate it into my work. We loved to draw when we were little, and my mom was always very resolute on me and my sisters working with quality tools: when we'd get back from school, she'd sharpen our crayons, make sure the Sharpies weren't dry, and give us piles of nice empty sheets to draw on. You'd think kids don't care about the types of tools they use, but I think it had a huge effect (on us)! I also think she was mostly encouraging us to draw because it would be the only thing that would keep my sister and I quiet for hours on end – we were quite the little rascals otherwise!

Stamp design for the Finnish Post, inspired by the architecture in Helsinki.

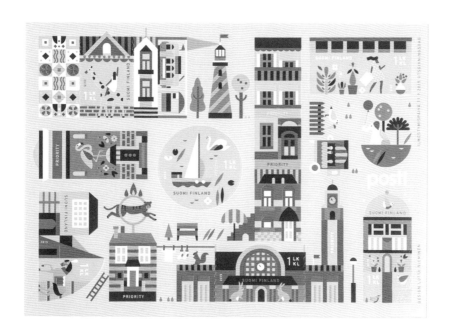

DESIGN{H}ERS

Olimpia Zagnoli

"Observe, be curious, disagree, explore the inside and outside of what it means to be human for you."

A creative female-type person born into an artistic family in Milano, Olimpia Zagnoli drives a Vespa and wears large round glasses. She also can – and does – draw like an ambidextrous octopus. Armed with prodigious skills and a doppio espresso, she has been called a "millennial stronza" by a certain green-eyed monster (i.e. the writer of this profile, Laurie Rosenwald). Although she will admit to being influenced by Bruno Munari, Paul Rand, and the other usual suspects, she creates super fresh shapely shapes and completely new voluptuous forms in her own clean palette of brights and darks.

OLIMPIA ZAGNOLI

↗ **Italia**
Cover for Big Mamma's guide to Italian restaurants and cafes in 2017.

↑ **Apple**
Campaign for the opening of the Apple Piazza Liberty Store in 2018.

Q: **What would you like to achieve through your work?**

A: Freedom. The freedom to live the way I want and to say the things that I want to say.

Q: **Where do you see the future of women in design?**

A: I see it everywhere.

Q: **How can one become more creative?**

A: I don't think the goal should be to become MORE creative. I think we should all become better observers. Too many times, we use words that we have heard before, we think things that others have thought before, and we draw in styles we've seen before. Being creative is the exercise of forgetting all that for a second, imagining a new set of possibilities and connections, and finding a new way to relate to the world on our terms. So I guess the tip would be: Observe, be curious, disagree, and explore the inside and outside of what it means to be human for you.

Q: **Who are the women who inspire you?**

A: All the women who have found a way to navigate the social limits of their times to concentrate on a purpose, whether it was the right to vote or simply find a room of their own.

Q: **What do you love about being a woman?**

It's the only thing I know so I have to make the best out of it.

Q: **Name the proudest moment(s) of your life.**

A: I'm proud of myself everyday. From the most stupid little things to the big existential ones. And I think I deserve a candy for all of them.

Q: **What brings you joy?**

A: Rock'n'roll.

OLIMPIA ZAGNOLI

Illustrations for a series of t-shirts, sweatshirts, and accessories, for Prada's 2018 Spring / Summer Collection.

DESIGN{H}ERS

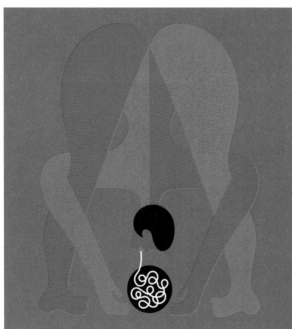

↗ How to Eat Spaghetti Like A Lady
Artworks for solo exhibition at Antonio Colombo Gallery in 2017.

DESIGN{H}ERS

Photo: Amelia Stanwix

Beci Orpin is a creative practitioner whose work occupies a space between illustration, design, and craft. Besides running a freelance studio to cater to a wide range of clients, she also exhibits her work locally and internationally, having authored four D.I.Y books and one children's title. Her work is described as colourful, graphic, bold, feminine, and dream-like.

↙ UNATTAINABLE RAINBOWS
Artworks for an exhibition at Lamington Drive Gallery, Melbourne, in 2017, including 'BECI Sculpture', 'Unhappiness Boutique', and 'Confession Booth'. Photos: Tatanja Ross

DESIGN{H}ERS

→ OUT OF BOUNDS with
Carla McRae
Artworks entitled 'Steady Up'
and 'Follow Through' for an
exhibition at Boom Gallery,
Geelong, in 2017.

↑ Business Card
Digital drawing as a self-initiated project.

← Untitled
Digital drawing for a painting for the Matter Arts charity show
in 2018.

"I think better creativity comes from feeding your brain with good experiences. Travelling, visiting galleries and gardens, meeting interesting people, eating good food, and listening to new music are all experiences which help my creativity."

→ **Matilda**
Digital drawing for a painting for the Terra Oztralis exhibition at Outré Gallery in 2018.

Q: What would you like to achieve through your work?

A: Optimism, empathy, and positivity.

Q: Where do you see the future of women in design?

A: Stronger and stronger.

Q: Could you please share some tips on how to become more creative?

A: I think better creativity comes from feeding your brain with good experiences. Travelling, visiting galleries and gardens, meeting interesting people, eating good food, and listening to new music are all experiences which help my creativity.

Q: Who are the women who inspire you?

A: My mother is very inspiring to me – she is a selfless hard worker and has always been a great feminist role model. There are a long list of females creatives whom I look to for inspiration – Sister Corita Kent, Tove Jansson, Miranda July, Ray Eames, Nathalie Du Pasquier, Patricia Urquiola, just to name a few. Plus, I am surrounded by an excellent group of female friends who inspire me daily.

Q: What do you love about being a woman?

A: I think being woman gives me a different viewpoint and approach to work and life.

Q: Name the proudest moment(s) of your life.

A: The birth of my children.

Q: What brings you joy?

A: Drawing in my sketchbook, making things, and my family.

↖ OLD / NEW / MADE / FOUND
Photographed collages on Metro tunnel hoardings for John Holland, City of Melbourne, in 2017.

LOOK DEEP

LOOK DEEP

Shyama Golden

After a decade of working in graphic and interactive design, independent visual artist Shyama Golden is currently focusing her practice on figurative art from her base in Brooklyn; complementing her formal training in studio art. Her meticulous style is as colourful and full of character as it is thoughtful and powerful. While oils are her preferred medium, Shyama also works digitally on the iPad Pro for the ability to create seamless patterns and looping animations.

↑ **Self Portrait**
Digital painting for personal work.

← **Women's March Poster**
Artwork to commemorate the one-year anniversary
of the Women's March for the Washington Post.

Q: What would you like to achieve through your work?

A: I hope to make people think, and step out of their daily lives for a moment to consider things in a new way.

Q: Where do you see the future of women in design?

A: There has been a large proportion of women in design for at least my whole lifetime, but in the future, we will see them get more credit and recognition for their work, and see more women rise to to the top of their fields.

Q: How can one become more creative?

A: Keep trying things you believe to be impossible. When you prove yourself wrong even some of those times, you will gain the confidence to try bolder and crazier things that few others will be doing.

Q: Who are the women who inspire you?

A: My mother, first of all. She is an incredibly selfless person, but has an independent spirit and doesn't care what anyone thinks. Being kind, and not giving a f*ck is an excellent combination that usually only comes with age (although some have been able to cultivate this earlier in life). A few others who fall into this category: Arundhati Roy, Amy Sherald, Frida Kahlo, Amrita Sher-Gil, Alice Neel.

Q: What do you love about being a woman?

A: I can't safely generalise any one thing that all women have in common, but empathy is something we have a tendency towards. Empathy is a superpower that is essential to a designer.

Q: Name the proudest moment(s) of your life.

A: It's not exactly one moment, but when I realised I was finally doing what I'm supposed to be doing on this planet, that was a wonderful feeling.

Q: What brings you joy?

A: Spending time with the people I love brings me the greatest joy, but the satisfaction of having found my calling and making a living out of it is the ultimate privilege. I am grateful for it all.

SHYAMA GOLDEN

↖ Female Portraits
Artworks for various clients and personal work.

DESIGN{H}ERS

↑ Arundhati
Illustration of Indian activist and writer Arundhati Roy for Atlantic
Magazine's July / August 2017 issue. Art Direction: Zak Bickel

→ Thillini
Digital drawing for personal work.

"Keep trying things you believe to be impossible."

DESIGN{H}ERS

Maricor/Maricar

Maricor/Maricar are twin sisters who love puns and specialise in hand-embroidered visuals and custom lettering. Graphic designers and animation directors in their previous lives, they both took their first stab at embroidery illustration for an animated music video and have never looked back. Since setting up their creative studio in 2010, they have won various awards for their intricate and whimsical work, including an RYD award from the British Council Australia and a Young Guns award by the ADC.

↖ **Painting with Thread**
Embroidered artwork for a private commission.

"We hope that there is more equality in the world in all facets, not just for women in design."

↖ **She Lights Up the Night**
Mixed media paint and embroidered artwork for the
She Lights Up The Night group exhibition in support of
Refuge, UK, in 2017.

DESIGN{H}ERS

← Don't Worry Baby
Embroidered artwork for the Material Edge group show in 2014.

↘ Love
Embroidered artwork for a private commission.

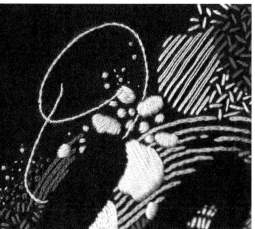

→ The Streets of Barangaroo
Illustrations for a 2017 campaign highlighting different aspects of the Barangaroo precinct for the Houston Group.

DESIGN{H}ERS

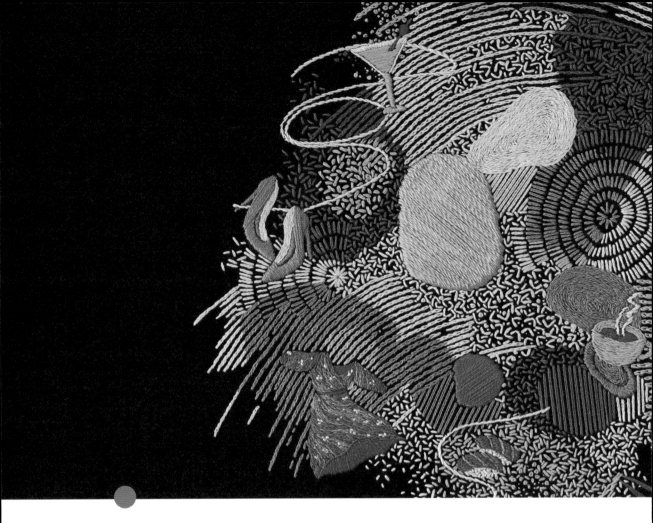

Q: What would you like to achieve through your work?

A: We want to create work that makes people take a second look. A lot of stimuli today is fast-paced and disposable, whereas embroidery is a slow process – it's tangible. We love getting lost in crafting the details and we hope that this experience is mirrored when people view our work.

Q: Where do you see the future of women in design?

A: This is a hard question. We hope that there is more equality in the world in all facets, not just for women in design. The world seems like a very different place now, and we hope that it's a chance to move forward.

Q: How can one become more creative?

A: We often go through phases of feeling creatively unmotivated and it feels like a bit of a slog. Spending a bit of time loosening up with doodles/sketches/studies and experiments helps me get out of a funk. Also, sometimes, enriching your soul and imagination by enjoying time away from the studio helps. Walking and actually seeing what's around you.

Q: Who are the women who inspire you?

A: Our mum, aunts and grandmothers, Sarah Illenberger, Beci Orpin.

Q: What do you love about being a woman?

A: I often feel too juvenile to call myself a woman, but I love my three children and still feel a huge sense of wonder that they came from me.

Q: Name the proudest moment(s) of your life.

A: Besides giving birth to my children, it would be: selling my first artwork, and being invited to the Buckingham Palace.

Q: What brings you joy?

A: A really good bowl of pho, discovering hidden gardens down different paths to places I always go to, interesting plants, lazy brunches with friends, and dancing with my partner and kids.

↑ **The Streets of Barangaroo**
Illustrations for a 2017 campaign highlighting different aspects of
the Barangaroo precinct for the Houston Group.

◉ SAN FRANCISCO / BROOKLYN

Jessica Hische

Jessica Hische is a lettering artist and author living in Oakland, California. She was raised in Hazleton, Pennsylvania, and received a BFA in Graphic and Interactive Design from Tyler School of Art, Temple University. After cutting her professional teeth working for Louise Fili, she started her one-woman studio in 2009 and has been operating independently since, creating work for clients like Wes Anderson, Starbucks, and Apple. She has received numerous awards including being named as one of Forbes's 30 Under 30, an ADC Young Gun, and a New Visual Artist by Print magazine. In 2018, she released her first children's book, 'Tomorrow I'll be Brave', which became a New York Times Best Seller.

Q: What would you like to achieve through your work?

A: First and foremost, I like to make people happy—whether that's a client, the audience for a piece, or just myself. I like to make work that is fun, warm, and light-hearted. I love making people smile with my work, or making them feel warm and fuzzy in some way.

Q: Where do you see the future of women in design?

A: I hope to see more women in prominent leadership positions within the design world and also more women talking about balancing working as a designer and motherhood. I hope, more and more, that people are celebrated not just for their extreme hustle but for finding a healthy balance between life and work, staying creative while also staying...human.

Q: How can one become more creative?

A: Get enough sleep, drink enough water, look away from Instagram and everyone's curated lives (seeing amazing work can be as intimidating as it can be motivating), and give yourself the space to make work that you are uniquely drawn to, not work that's in response to trends or what you think clients are looking for. Walks are helpful. Therapy is immensely helpful. Inane production work can be helpful. Anything that gets you unstuck, out of (or into) your head, and starting on something rather than being intimidated about starting.

Q: Who are the women who inspire you?

A: So many! Within the design and illustration world—Tina Roth Eisenberg for her insane ability to manage multiple businesses, be engaging and warm online, but also draw boundaries professionally. Debbie Millman, who is just an amazing person—so generous with her time and self on top of being so talented. Gemma O'Brien for somehow doing all the things that she does while being on planes half the year. Louise Fili for all the mentorship she gave me over the years. And I just have too many amazing inspiring lady friends to even name! There are of course the more mainstream celebrity ladies too—Michelle Obama, Amy Poehler and Tina Fey, Beyoncé, et al.

Q: What do you love about being a woman?

A: I think one of the main things I love about being a woman is feeling like I have both the ability (and permission) to really work to understand myself from the inside out. I think women can be naturally more attuned to stuff going on within their bodies and minds (monthly cycles and hormonal patterns help with that immensely), which can lead to having a more complete understanding of how you as an individual operate. Men can definitely get in touch with themselves, but I think it can be more difficult for them—both because it's not been a societally encouraged behaviour for so long (things are changing on that front) and because they don't have a monthly pattern to pay attention to that helps them calibrate themselves. Knowing yourself deeply, I believe, is the key to happiness in life—to finding the right path to follow, right choices to make, etc.

Q: Name the proudest moment(s) of your life.

A: 1. Being named top portfolio of my graduating class. I worked SO HARD throughout school, and it meant so much to be recognised by my teachers. Even if I hadn't won the top prize, they encouraged me so much throughout my time there that I think I still would have walked away at graduation with just as much pride.

2. Seeing my work on the big screen. When Moonrise Kingdom came out, we bought 40 seats at a local art house movie theatre and invited friends to come see the movie with us. When my name came up in the credits as title designer and all of my friends started clapping and cheering, I cried my eyes out.

3. When I was able to completely turn around a project that was going south (the client was on the verge of firing me because we had a huge miscommunication early in the project) and I was able to win them back over after giving 110% to a new round of work.

4. Anytime my kids do something new and challenging and look at me with happy anticipation in their faces and we celebrate together.

Q: What brings you joy?

A: First and foremost, seeing happiness and/or pride in my children's faces. It's a different kind of joy, one that I can't achieve on my own or through work. Second, hearing that my work or words helped someone in some way, big or small. I hear from people all the time (through email) who have seen me speak, read my articles, or encountered one of my projects and I was able to inspire them, dig them out of a creative rut, or just brighten their day. One email can give me a jolt of creative fuel for a whole week.

DESIGN{H}ERS

"Knowing yourself deeply, I believe, is the key to happiness in life."

→ **Oprah's 15 Things**
Artwork in celebration of O Magazine's 15th year of publication.
Art Direction: Jessica Weit

↓ **Snacks Quarterly**
Artwork to accompany a 2014 interview in Snacks Quarterly magazine.
Art Direction: Brad Simon

↗ **Starbucks**
Lettering artwork in a 2014 advertising campaign for Starbucks in collaboration with the BBDO creative team, including Dennis Lim, Rachel Frederick, Jr., Alia Robers, and John Clang.

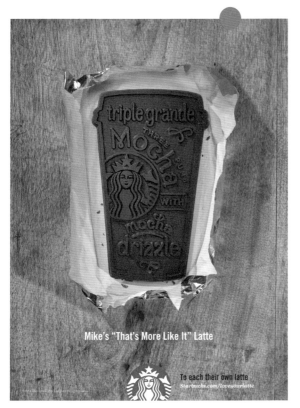

Mike's "That's More Like It" Latte

To each their own latte
Starbucks.com/loveyourlatte

Rachel's "All Better Now" Latte

To each their own latte
Starbucks.com/loveyourlatte

Jessica's "Got My Groove Back" Latte

To each their own latte
Starbucks.com/loveyourlatte

Erin's "I So Deserve This" Latte

To each their own latte
Starbucks.com/loveyourlatte

DESIGN{H}ERS

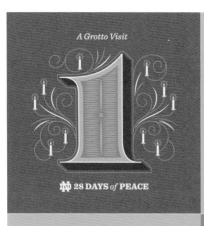

A Grotto Visit

ND 28 DAYS of PEACE

Thank a Public Servant

ND 28 DAYS of PEACE

Gone, but not Forgotten

ND 28 DAYS of PEACE

Our Story is Forgiveness

ND 28 DAYS of PEACE

Shake It Out

ND 28 DAYS of PEACE

The Peace of Silence

ND 28 DAYS of PEACE

Life Imitates Art, Art imitates Peace

ND 28 DAYS of PEACE

Ensure Domestic Tranquility

ND 28 DAYS of PEACE

Pray with Father Ted

ND 28 DAYS of PEACE

Hand on the Gift of Faith

ND 28 DAYS of PEACE

Saints Who Died for Peace

ND 28 DAYS of PEACE

Reach Out and Touch Someone

ND 28 DAYS of PEACE

The Sound of Silence — 4 — 28 DAYS of PEACE

Feed the Hungry — 5 — 28 DAYS of PEACE

Inspired Reading — 6 — 28 DAYS of PEACE

A Good Neighbor — 10 — 28 DAYS of PEACE

Make Me An Instrument of Peace — 11 — 28 DAYS of PEACE

Full of Grace — 12 — 28 DAYS of PEACE

Our Lady of Life — 16 — 28 DAYS of PEACE

I'll Pray for You — 17 — 28 DAYS of PEACE

To Sing is to Pray Twice — 18 — 28 DAYS of PEACE

Force for Good — 22 — 28 DAYS of PEACE

Our Lady of Life — 23 — 28 DAYS of PEACE

Work for Justice, Sow Peace — 24 — 28 DAYS of PEACE

↑ **28 Days of Peace**
Illustrations for an Advent calendar by the Notre Dam Alumni Association, in which each number is unique and related to a daily reflection or action leading up to Christmas Day 2016.
Art Direction: Kiley Loesch, Bill Gangluff

DESIGN{H}ERS

Camille Walala

A purveyor of powerfully positive digital print, Camille Walala is driven by the simple desire to put a smile on people's faces. Besides her popular textile-based range under her namesake brand founded in 2009, she is also involved in art direction, interior design, and pop-up restaurants, where her love for food and design comes to life. Counting the Memphis movement, Ndebele tribe, and op art master Vasarely among her influences, Camille's signature tribal pop style exudes a boundless energy that manifests itself best on social and show-stopping canvases – the bigger, the better.

Photo: Charles Emerson

↖ **Camille Walala x Industry City**
40m mural for WantedDesign Brooklyn's NYCxDESIGN festival programme in 2018. Images courtesy of Industry City.

DESIGN{H}ERS

→ **PLAY MORE: Camille Walala x Visual Magnetics**
Interactive mural / installation for WantedDesign Manhattan in 2018. Photo: Story and Gold

↓ **DREAM COME TRUE**
Mural for the Splice building, London.

CAMILLE WALALA

Q: What would you like to achieve through your work?

A: I would love for my work to be accessible to everyone. I want to bring the viewer a strong sense of joy and playfulness. I often try and imagine how I used to feel when I was a child when approaching projects. I want unadulterated happiness.

Q: Where do you see the future of women in design?

A: I think the future of women in design is going from strength to strength. I have many talented female friends who are becoming increasingly successful with their work. It's great to see this!

Q: How can one become more creative?

A: I think, as with anything, practice makes perfect. If you do a little bit of creative work everyday over time, you will learn what you like and don't like, and your knowledge will improve your work.

Q: Who are the women who inspire you?

A: I am very inspired by Sonia Delaunay, Bridget Riley, and Dr Esther Mahlangu.

Q: Name the proudest moment(s) of your life.

A: The proudest moment of my life was when I completed my very first mural on a building. The 'Dream Come True' building mural in Shoreditch, London, was the first of many giant murals. I will always remember how proud I felt when I completed that particular project.

Q: What brings you joy?

A: Eating cheese :)

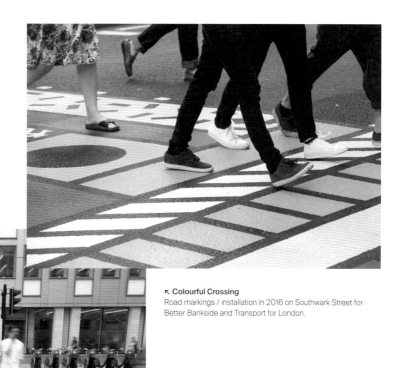

↖ Colourful Crossing
Road markings / installation in 2016 on Southwark Street for Better Bankside and Transport for London.

DESIGN{H}ERS

↘ **SALT x Camille Walala**
Interior design for the experience-led, sustainability-focused
SALT of Palmar hotel in Mauritius. Photos: Tekla Evelina Severin

DESIGN{H}ERS

↘ **WALALA x The Naked Heart Foundation**
Design work for the Fabulous Fund Fair in 2016 at The
Roundhouse, London. Photos: Dan Weill Photography

DESIGN{H}ERS

Leslie David

Photo: Lebruman

A French designer, art director, and illustrator who launched her multidisciplinary creative studio in 2009, Leslie David dedicates her work to creating holistic visual solutions. Passionate about finding the best ways to make content-driven visuals, she brings all aspects of branding to life across fashion, art, beauty, music, and culture through thoughtfully crafted print and digital implementations in her bold and eye-popping style. Always exploring a large spectrum of mediums from paintings to 3D-animated shapes, Leslie's powerful imagination and creativity in mixed media are apparent in all her projects as she seeks out new intriguing and exciting collaborations.

"I think we still have work to do in order to be able to get briefs and clients not targeted for women only."

Q: What would you like to achieve through your work?

A: My work translates my creative and artistic views of the world and of the things surrounding us in our everyday life. It provides me with a special understanding of the architecture, brands, and objects we don't necessarily pay attention to on a daily basis and helps me to picture specific moods and aesthetics. I would like to democratise great and well-made innovative designs through my work.

I try to find creative fulfilment and visual stimulation through our clients' constraints to provide new graphic proposals. I would also like to apprehend new artistic mediums as I don't want to settle and be trapped in one specific style or kind of design. This is why I like to have a studio: it allows me to work with different creatives, which is nurturing and stimulating.

Q: Where do you see the future of women in design?

A: Fortunately, women's status in design has evolved and is still going through big changes. When I was in school, I struggled to find a female role model in this business. I spent many years in art schools, and we were mostly girls, but when you looked at the industry, the studios around were only run by men! I finally found a few and ended up doing several internships with women designers, as I was looking for models. I wanted to understand how they were managing their time between their passions and their family life. I don't think this problem has been solved, but there are definitely more girls in the industry today. I think the world will keep evolving in this direction, and it's a good thing! However, I think we still have work to do to be able to get briefs and clients not targeted for women only. Hundreds of studios run by men work for brands targeting women, but the opposite isn't true. It's a shame that people still think we would be less legitimate to understand and work for brands targeting men.

Q: How can one become more creative?

A: My creativity comes from constant experimentation. I love trying new things, new mediums, new techniques, and new tools I wouldn't even have thought about. I like being really surprised by the result of just trying things out. Also, instead of looking on Pinterest, I try to dig my inspiration from old art books, old pictures, and lithographies to revisit things people have often forgotten about.

Q: Who are the women who inspire you?

A: My friends, who are funny, talented, and intelligent women. I am also deeply inspired by the three women who taught me so much when I did my first internships: Helena Ichbiah, Deanne Cheuk, and Sylvia Tournerie. If I had to cite a few more inspirations, I would definitely talk about Sonia Delaunay, Barbara Hulanicki, Judy Chicago, Shirley Jaffe, Nathalie Dupasquier, Björk, and many more!

Q: What do you love about being a woman?

A: I know how cliched this sounds (and I really don't want to reduce being a woman to this aspect of life, of course), but the one thing that really makes me happy about being a woman is maternity. Women have the power to live this amazing experience.

Q: Name the proudest moment(s) of your life

A: I honestly never thought I would one day be running my own studio when I started my career. Looking back, I think that the lack of female role models and representatives scared me into thinking that it wouldn't happen. I am really proud that I finally got here even if there are still plenty of things to do, to develop, and to grow!

Q: What brings you joy?

A: I won't be very original here, but I think we all know the recipe for a happy and healthy life. I like spending time with my daughter, cooking for family and friends, working on exciting projects, living new experiences, eating homemade recipes by my mum, travelling, and taking time for myself!

↘ Isabel Marant
Art direction and photography for a new collection by the French fashion house in 2018.
Photos: Aude Lebarbey / Set Design: Céline Corbineau

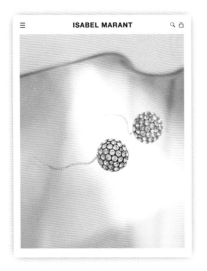

DESIGN{H}ERS

↗ **Jordan**
Art direction for Season of Her, a 2018 campaign featuring the first Air Jordan sneakers for women, in collaboration with Benjamin Vigliotta. Photos: Lara Giliberto / Styling: Dan Sablon / Set Design: Camille Lebourges / Make-up & Hair: les filles / Production: Rififi Production

REAL TALK #3
TO EXPERIMENT IS TO EVOLVE

↘

Yu Yah-Leng

REAL TALK #3 YU YAH-LENG @ FOREIGN POLICY DESIGN GROUP

Yu Yah-Leng

Co-founder, Foreign Policy Design Group

Foreign Policy Design Group in Singapore was co-founded by Yu Yah-Leng in 2007, following a journey of creative discovery in the USA. Equipped with a distinct visual style and a unique global perspective of design, she was driven to build a practice that could hold its own amongst the industry's top players at the time. Drawing on her own love for experimentation, Yah-Leng leads the studio by avoiding the conventional and predictable, foregrounding their work against a dynamic city which continues to be an epicentre of fresh ideas across different fields in Asia. Besides winning numerous accolades from various international design organisations, she has also been a speaker, design awards jury member, and the President of The Design Society in Singapore.

DESIGN{H}ERS

Yu Yah-Leng's journey into design as a student was far from conventional, unwittingly setting the course for her future studio's ascent. Initially enrolled in a science degree programme at a local university, it took a bicycle accident in her first year to make her realise that she was on the wrong path in life. Led by intuition and serendipidity, she soon found herself applying for courses in the USA without any concrete idea of what she was doing, and eventually ended up at Art Institute Boston even though it was not the preferred choice for foreign students at the time.

"I just fell in love with the city," she says fondly of the years at her alma mater. "I was a slightly older student compared to my classmates, who were also slightly older than average, and because we were more mature and kind of knew what we wanted in life, we were more disciplined. We were more active and fruitful too – organising events, going to exhibitions, visiting design studios and all that." Her prolificacy and resourcefulness also opened the door to early freelancing gigs, where she helped to produce various collaterals for a friend who was working at a print shop chain.

Taking every chance to grow, she then honed her skillsets at several places after she graduated with the dream of staying on in the country; hungry to learn the ropes of how a studio worked. Through sheer dedication, she landed a role in a tiny agency that gave her the opportunity to develop her HTML and multimedia knowledge. "The agency worked across lots of things – editorial design, school textbooks, annual reports, magazines – and because I had always been interested in technology, I volunteered one day to do a particular job that required web presence. (There were also) technology specialists from whom we could learn, elevate our website-making skills, and make kick-ass stuff." Following 9-11, the dot-com bubble burst and forced the agency to close down, but she remains optimistic about that low point in her life. "The good thing that came out of (that experience) was that my colleagues and I started to form our own little agencies to do our own thing(s)."

Although some time has passed since, Yah-Leng's love of learning and technology has not changed, and she still applies it to her design work. She believes that diving head-first into the deep end can more often be for good. "I was trained as a graphic designer in print, but multimedia was kind of huge if you were doing it back then. My first-ever job was not even for a graphic design position, but a multimedia position, so I actually went beyond what I was trained in. I also picked up HTML on my own. I learned that it is very important to have different skillsets, even though you might not become an expert in them. It is also important to understand function or how things work, like how a website can be built, so that you can apply design in the best way."

Shaped by her past, her philosophy of constant evolution continues to guide her methodology and aptitude for change in the present. "I always try not to take a very silo view when approaching design because of my different experiences in different firms. The last digital design agency I worked with was very technology-driven, so it pushed me to always be updated with what is out there, and how people are applying design to technology and vice versa. I found it all really interesting."

As an evolving hub that continuously strives to reinvent itself, Singapore, her home country, forms the perfect backdrop for her creative endeavours today; with concepts that seamlessly blend the East and the West, with the past and the present. When she started Foreign Policy Design Group upon her return from the USA, however, things were not quite as vibrant and diverse. "The scene was still very much dominated by international advertising agencies and brand agencies, but as we moved along, it all became very exciting as we began seeing a lot more good work with global standards." Although the city is known as the 'Little Red Dot' among locals due to its size, she is able to see the bigger picture, giving credit where it is due for what it has become creatively and culturally. "I would like to say that the government did a good job promoting Singapore in certain ways. We also have the opportunity to travel a lot for work, studies, or leisure because of our geography, so I think Singaporeans are quite well travelled, well-heeled, and well-exposed."

For a woman who has risen through the ranks of running her own studio, Yah-Leng has seen the ups and downs of trying to be seen and heard amongst the giants in the wider industry. While everything from public perceptions and company policies used to be more insular and conservative in nature, the future looks promising for the next generation, especially in terms of support and mentorship for women in design.

"For the longest time, they have been trying to give the President's Design Award (www.designsingapore.org/presidents-design-award) to a woman, and they finally did in 2017 – even though she is an architect and not a graphic designer. In Singapore, women's voices are actually quite loud now, and my peers have been encouraging me to do something for the scene." As President of The Design Society (http://designsociety.sg) in 2018, she hopes to be more active in the coming year. "I am seeing more and more women designers coming up, so I am not really worried about gender inequality – which is a good thing. There are many talented, illustrious girls waiting in the wings."

...ed br...
...ll rump of pork, succotash.
...ed chilli, fried duck egg
Chilli prawns, grilled oak leaf, fennel,
avocado and green goddess dressing

PLA...
two cg...
cherry...
fried b...

6 × More...
Beef tart...
dripping...
Half roas...
nasturtiu...
Roasted...
egg, blac...
Heritage...
flower, so...
Smoked...
skin, soy...

ARE YOU LONESOME TONIGHT

NIGHT

English peas, broad beans, fregola,
mozzarella and strawberry salad

Smoked chicken Caesar salad, baco...
Berkswell cheese

Dry aged pork...
peas, wild...

SIDES

MAINS

SALADS & SANDWICHES

STARTERS

DESSERTS

BREAKFAST
BREAKFAST

BREAKFAST

STACK O' PANCAKES
buttermilk pancakes, bacon, maple syrup   12.—

BIRD FOOD
chia seed bircher muesli, dried berries, coconut milk   11.—

FRENCH TOAST
buttermilk pancakes, bacon, maple syrup   11.—

GREEN EGGS AND HAM
buttermilk pancakes, bacon, maple syrup   15.—

EAT YER VEGGIES
buttermilk pancakes, bacon, maple syrup   12.—

SWEETS FOR YO...

PLATTER   18.—

↗ One Night Only
Visual identity and interior design development for
One Night Only, a modern diner in Singapore.

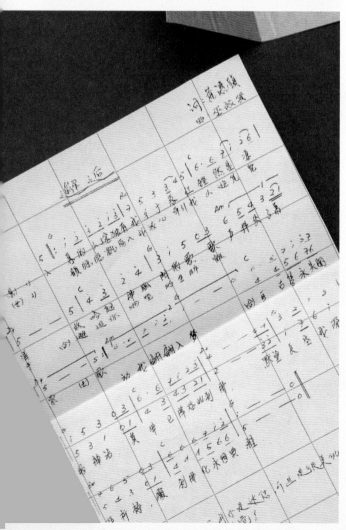

In recent years, she has also observed a curious number of professionals that have quit their jobs to run start-ups such as cafés or fashion concept stores, a phenomenon that has led to some interesting branding projects for the studio. "These people are not trivial; they take it all quite seriously. They know the game, and that design is important. They know that their store needs to look good, with the right branding and experience. They do their homework, know the right design studios, and get their help to make things happen, which is how studios like ours get the opportunity to work with them."

Besides the welcomed challenge of more complex design briefs, she also embraces the increasing levels of competition which have helped to push their work standards higher. "Designers in Singapore are more hungry, and I think it is quite healthy for the creative scene overall – even among the indie bands here! Interesting creatives are just popping up, and it really is a great time for us now. I hope it gets even better," she enthuses.

After years in the business, Yah-Leng is still raring to go, but as with all good leaders who have built a solid practice, she juggles with the hard questions regarding its future. Following the studio's tenth anniversary in 2017, she and her team have been asking themselves what they would like to do next, and are conscious of needing to stay relevant. They remain adamant about not being boxed into any particular discipline or sector, hoping to pave the path towards new directions.

"As a design studio and a designer myself, we need to be able to grasp what is happening today and tomorrow because we are the reflection of the future," she says passionately. "We need to keep reevaluating ourselves and figure out how to innovate and pivot for the next ten years, and do something slightly different and exciting. With all this new technology like AI, will we be able to harness it? Is print really dead? We are still big on print, so how can we augment tech that is supposed to 'kill' print? We will always be thinking about it."

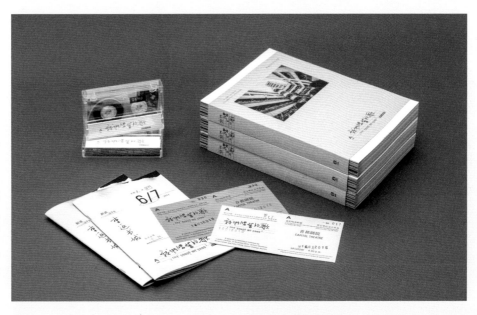

↗ **The Songs We Sang**
Book design as part of a documentary by Eva Tang in 2018, chronicling a uniquely Singaporean heritage.

DESIGN{H}ERS

Looking through their portfolio, one would be hard-pressed to find cookie-cutter solutions, with every project mirroring her emphasis on purpose. As striking as their work can be, there is also a beautiful sense of subtlety. "I do not believe in forcing my clients to 'take on' my style, because I should not 'be' a style. I believe in adapting, because this approach resonates with them better, and the results will have longevity. We work together, and it is very important for us to understand our clients because the work is not even for them, but for their customers, so they also have to understand that they cannot impose their own personalities too much."

That said, she is aware that some of their strongest projects emerge from close collaboration with their clients, and believes that the right chemistry can make or break a project. She resonates with those who give them a lot of trust and are visionaries who are not afraid to take some risks in design, even though she admits that Asian clients tend to play it safe.

"It is a quite a typical mindset to have. However, when a client goes 'let's do something different – I really do not want to be conventional, predictable, or the usual in the industry', then we know that this is who we want to work with. We are very lucky to have met people like these. It is important to embrace something new or something you are not comfortable with, because it can add to your perspective and approach in whatever you are trying to do next time."

Although the act of transforming oneself or one's own studio can be an uphill task, there seems to be nothing that could stop Yah-Leng as she forges her own path forward, with her instincts and innovative spirit leading the way.

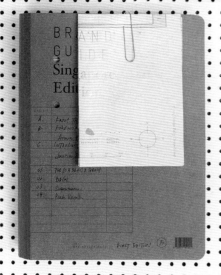

↗ Brand Guide: Singapore Edition
Design work for the Brand Guide series in 2015 by Foreign Policy Design Group.

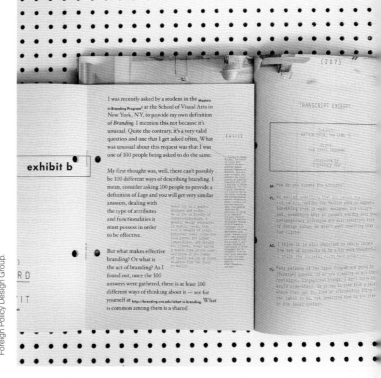

"As a design studio, we need to be able to grasp what is happening today and tomorrow because we are a reflection of the future."

Roanne Adams

RoAndCo is an award-winning creative studio bringing thought, relevance, and style to forward-thinking fashion, beauty, tech, and lifestyle brands. Founded in 2006 by its creative director, Roanne Adams, the team works intuitively to pinpoint the most essential, visceral quality with which to tell a brand's story. As both a strategic and creative resource to clients at every step of the process, Roanne aligns inspiration, business objectives, and story-telling into powerful experiences through the studio with her distinct skill for distilling brands into their most succinct forms.

↘ **ROMANCE JOURNAL: Issue 02 – Resistance**
Editorial design and art direction for the second issue of Romance
Journal in 2017, which features a curation of today's most thoughtful
and powerful women activists, entrepreneurs, and artists. Founder &
Creative Director: Roanne Adams / Contributing Editor: Dana Covit
/ Portrait Photography: Samantha Casolari, Alex John Beck / Still
Life Photography: Scottie Cameron / Prop Stylist: Sonia Rentsch /
Retouching: Amanda Yanez

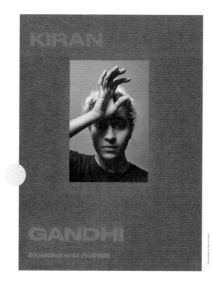

KIRAN GANDHI

Musician and Activist

KIRAN GANDHI

Kiran Gandhi is an activist and musician performing under the name Madame Gandhi. After touring with M.I.A. in 2015 Kiran ran the London Marathon while bleeding freely on her period to spark a conversation about the stigmatization of women's bodies in different cultures worldwide. Since then, Kiran has partnered with women's health organizations to improve access to affordable and safe menstrual care. Through her music and activism, Kiran's mission is to elevate and celebrate women's voices.

88—89

ROMANCE JOURNAL

The past is female, the present is female, the future is female. I think the future is for all genders. I think the future is inclusive. The future is for everybody. Every damn body!

28—29

CARMEN PEREZ

Executive Director of The Gathering for Justice and Co-Founder of Justice League NYC

CARMEN PEREZ

Carmen Perez is the Executive Director of The Gathering for Justice and co-founder of Justice League NYC. Named by *TIME* Magazine as among the 100 most influential people of 2017, Carmen has dedicated her life to advocacy and civil rights issues, with particular focus on mass incarceration and criminal justice system reform over the course of the last two decades. She served as National Co-Chair for the 2017 Women's March on Washington, and remains a fearless, yet truly honest leader as Treasurer of the Women's March Organization.

14—15

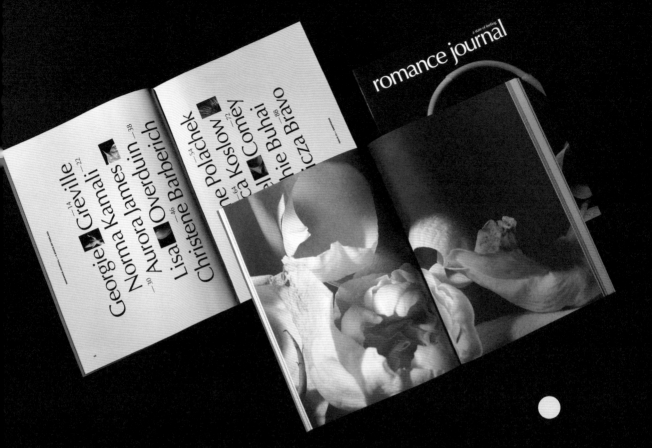

romance journal

a state of feeling

FEATURING

Georgie Greville
Norma Kamali
Aurora James
Lisa Overduin
~~Christene Barberich~~

roman

March 30th, 2017

HOSTED BY

Roanne Adams
Georgie Greville
Lisa Overduin
Janieza Bravo
Jessica Koslow

↙ ROMANCE JOURNAL: Issue 01 – Emotions
Editorial design and art direction for the first issue of Romance Journal in 2017, which is devoted to exploring the truth and raising the collective consciousness. Founder & Creative Director: Roanne Adams / Contributing Editor: Eviana Hartman / Photography: Robin Stein / Floral Design: Britta Walsworth – These Colours / Retouching: Tomika Davis

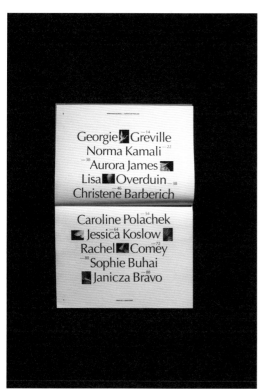

DESIGN{H}ERS

↓ **Young Guns 15**
Visual identity, print collateral, and award cube design for The
One Club for Creativity's Young Guns awards ceremony in 2017.
Society Awards: Cube Production

"We just need to find our
balance in this crazy world.
We need to be in touch with
ourselves and nature, and
then we can thrive."

Q: What would you like to achieve through your work?

A: When I ventured out on my own to start RoAndCo back in 2006, I set out to bring conceptual branding and art direction to small start-up brands in the fashion, art, and lifestyle industries. I wanted to connect with forward-thinking clients; creating beautiful and smart designs for them. Back then, I felt like good graphic design (the kind that merged style with strategy) was really under-appreciated in the USA. All of the best design I was seeing was coming out of England. Everything from British album covers to their street signage was just superior to what was coming out of NYC. Looking back on what I set out to achieve then, I'd like to think that I helped to usher a new wave of graphic design appreciation into New York over the past decade...with the help of many other designers and art directors of course! The sort of branding work we've been doing at RoAndCo for the past decade is now very common. NYC has become a graphic design mecca of sorts. And thankfully, American brands see the importance of strategic brand thinking as well as good design style.

Today, what I would like to achieve through our work is deeper meaning; not just beautiful, strategic design using conceptual ideas and strategic thinking, but using design to harness good in the world. Projects like Romance Journal reflect that by uplifting women, bringing marginalised voices to the forefront, exploring creativity, wellness, balance and power, etc.

I'm working on co-creating a future for both RoAndCo and Romance Journal with my team. We're exploring what it means to lead through our emotions and how to create meaningful design that also allows us, the creators, to feel creatively fulfilled. For our clients, it's about helping them connect to their higher purpose and use their platform/business/product/service to help the world in some way. These days, everybody needs to be creating work that has meaning and holds true to a higher purpose. It's not just about making money. I want it to evoke emotion and connect people to their truth, to their higher purpose.

Q: Where do you see the future of women in design?

A: It's crazy to think that only 11% of Creative Directors in the advertising industry are female. I feel very lucky that I was able to create a successful design practice and appoint myself to the role that I have today. It takes other women a lifetime to get there in a male-dominated agency. Women are inherently creative. Women are inherently powerful. Women are great leader and mentors. The future for women in design holds SO much potential. We all have creative powers, and women need other female mentors to help them get there. Women who are in positions like mine need to help other women unleash their creative potential and feel empowered to do what they truly believe is right. I think my generation of women were/are still people-pleasing. We're working on getting to our truth everyday, and feeling free to express it through design.

Q: How can one become more creative?

A: Be still. Listen to your inner voice. Carve time out to meditate on your creative ideas. Don't let emails and meetings cloud your entire day and disrupt your creative flow. Be kind to yourself.

Q: Who are the women who inspire you?

A: There are way too many to list! Björk, Madonna, Kate Bush, Vanessa Beecroft, Rachel Comey, Piera Gelardi, Phoebe Philo, Frida Kahlo, Hilma af Klint, all of the women I work with at RoAndCo.

Q: What do you love about being a woman?

A: We have the power to manifest anything. We're beautiful, emotional creatures. I'm not going to lie, I've lived a very privileged life. I've worked for it, but I've also gotten so many incredible opportunities. Perhaps because I'm a woman, and because other women who own or run businesses have wanted to work with a female-led agency. It's been interesting to acknowledge that being a woman has brought me nothing but success in life. While I know this is rare, I'm very grateful for it. Now, I want to help other women thrive in their careers and in life. We just need to find our balance in this crazy world. We need to be in touch with ourselves and nature, and then we can thrive.

Q: Name the proudest moment(s) of your life.

A: The day I started RoAndCo. The morning I gave birth to my daughter, Phaedra. The day I decided to not shut down RoAndCo when we went through a challenging time, and instead decided to not only keep RoAndCo going but to also start Romance Journal as a creative outlet for myself. The day I launched Romance Journal Issue 1. The night I gave birth to my son, Orion.

Q: What brings you joy?

A: Creation, connection, travel, getting into the FLOW, and spending time with my family and friends.

DESIGN{H}ERS

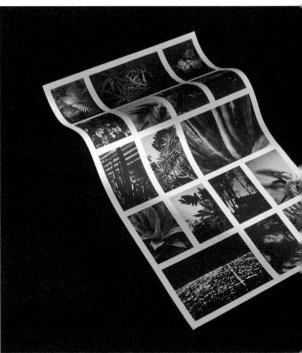

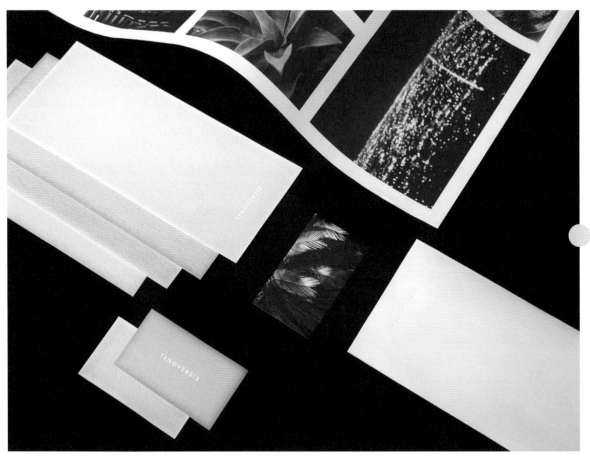

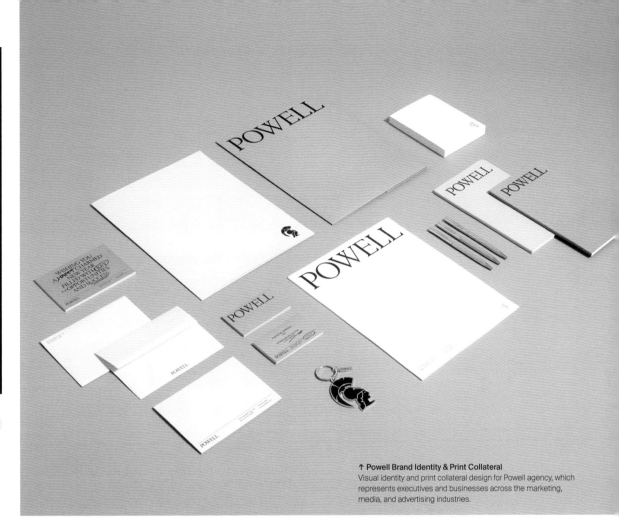

↑ Powell Brand Identity & Print Collateral
Visual identity and print collateral design for Powell agency, which represents executives and businesses across the marketing, media, and advertising industries.

DESIGN{H}ERS

Vanessa Eckstein

Specialising in brand identities and experiences, packaging design, exhibition design as well as editorial design, Blok Studio was founded in 1998 by Vanessa Eckstein. The studio collaborates with thinkers, creators, companies, and brands from around the world on projects that blend cultural awareness and a love for art as well as humanity to advance society and businesses alike. Whether she is designing or developing a book, a digital experience, or a new product line, she seeks to create indelible experiences that profoundly move people through her work.

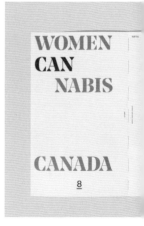

Q: What would you like to achieve through your work?

A: I am an idealist at heart. It is a character trait that I simply can't escape, guiding most of the decisions I make and the way I understand design and life. I believe in the power of design to effect change, to question society, to push frontiers; but this does not always have to be on a grand scale. Many times, it is at its most powerful when it challenges preconceptions, reframes a story, or inspires someone's belief of what is possible.

Q: Where do you see the future of women in design?

A: Everywhere! We stand on the shoulders of many great women designers and artists before us, and we should help guide the generation after. Equality, like freedom, should never be a privilege or a need, but a fundamental right. And, as with many other voices in our society, we bring with us a diversity, a point of view, a narrative, and a sensibility that is not defined by our gender but by our own personal experiences.

Q: How can one become more creative?

A: Inspiration is a continuous movement, not a special occasion. Everything we encounter from art to music – the colours at a market, the textures of a sculpture, the words of a poet, the subtle details of a building – all adds to our souls and transforms as time goes by. This is our reservoir of beauty and awe, of thoughtfulness or playfulness. We feed from it in ways that are truly unknown to me except that I recognise the moment when it all falls into place, and the project takes shape or the idea finds its reason. Openness and curiosity is the guiding force, to have the patience to listen well, to see clearly, to appreciate the extraordinary in the ordinary, to learn the unfamiliar.

Q: Who are the women who inspire you?

A: Many women have inspired me throughout my life, from renowned artists like Louise Bourgeois and writers like Susan Sontag and Virginia Woolf, to women in my life like Carol Wells, the director and founder of the Centre for the Study of Political Graphics and my mother, Daphne Eckstein – a true artist in her own right who decided never to part with her art no matter how much money she was offered. Each one of these women has carved a space for themselves. Many times, against all odds, against governments, societal preconceptions, monocultures, and a rhetoric that did not support their art nor their voice. Each one stood for what they believed in, following their own path, doing nothing other than what they did. I admire those with the relentless spirit to pursue their own truth and, in doing so, shift the paradigm.

Q: What do you love about being a woman?

A: I think as a woman, we are connected to our spiritual selves in ways that our senses are heightened. This is always clear to me by our acute intuition, our connection to the intangible, and many times, the magical. Being a mother is the fullest expression of this connectivity and its influence pours into my own creative self. It has inspired me to see the world from a very different perspective, to find the edges and rethink it all from there.

Q: Name the proudest moment(s) of your life.

A: The proudest moment of my life was the one where I surrendered to life as it revealed itself in all its beauty: the day I had my children. There is no other moment that channelled all the creative spirit I carry as profoundly and as expansive as that day.

Q: What brings you joy?

A: I find joy in so many things – from the everyday enjoyment of a delicious piece of chocolate to the expansiveness of a great work of art. I find joy in the elusive moment of beauty, the words of a writer that made me wonder, or even my kids' excitement over the simplest of discoveries. I find joy in the sensuality of a typeface, the power of colour, the presence of friendship, or the longing of something so far I still cannot reach.

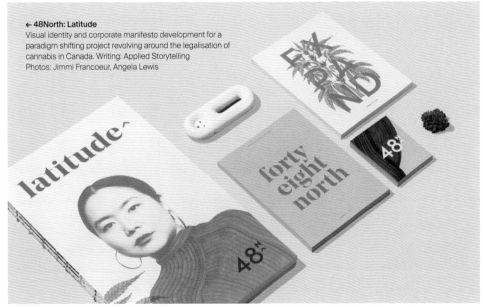

← 48North: Latitude
Visual identity and corporate manifesto development for a paradigm shifting project revolving around the legalisation of cannabis in Canada. Writing: Applied Storytelling
Photos: Jimmi Francoeur, Angela Lewis

OCTOBER
16
VDC
FREE
AND ALL S
CHE
SI
Your
March on Washington
Sunday, April 9, 1989
is a
Support Legal A
Birth Control
and Women's Right
battleground
On April 26 the Supreme Court will hear a case which the Bush Admi

> "Equality, like freedom, should never be a privilege or a need but a fundamental right."

↑ CSPG
Visual identity design for the Centre for the Study of Political Graphics, depicting one of humanity's oldest and greatest endeavours: the struggle against justice.

DESIGN{H}ERS

→ **superkül**

Visual identity and collateral design for one of Canada's
leading architecture firms, featuring an interplay between
process, colour, shape, and materiality.

↙ Modern Recreation
Visual identity and collateral design for a purveyor of coffee beans from some of the world's best small-batch roasters.

DESIGN{H}ERS

↖ The Broadview
Visual identity and collateral design for The Broadview
Hotel, a historic architectural landmark reimagined as a
luxury boutique accommodation.

DESIGN(H)ERS

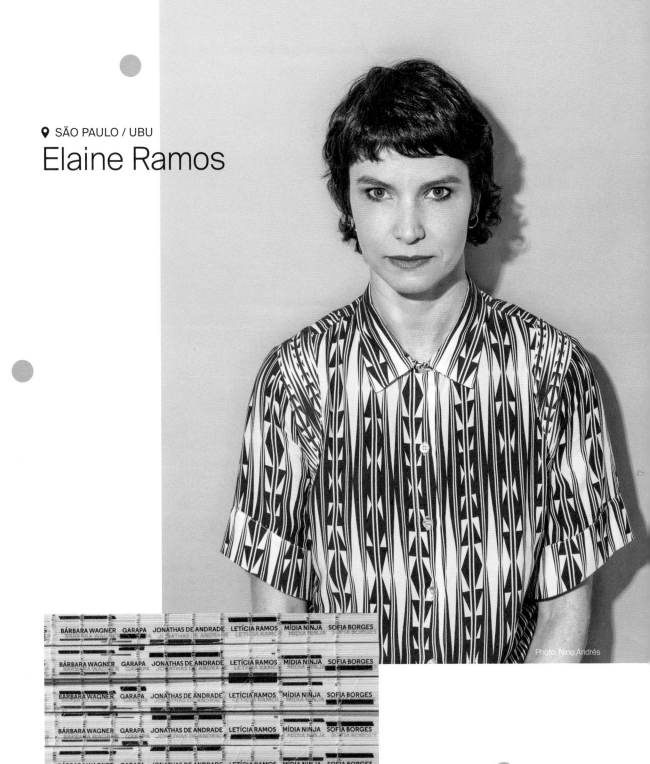

Elaine Ramos

Photo: Nino Andrés

Formerly an art director at Cosac Naify where she designed hundreds of books, Elaine Ramos is a co-founder of the publishing house, Ubu, and currently runs her own design studio in São Paulo. Besides having translated fundamental titles such as Meggs' History of Graphic Design, she has also been dedicating herself to the research and preservation of local design. From 2008 to 2011, Elaine was involved in constructing the seminal Brazilian Graphic Design Timeline, where she surveyed more than 1,600 images to build a panorama showcasing two centuries of local design production.

"I hope women can reach equality in terms of professional opportunities and remuneration."

↙ Corpo a Corpo
Catalogue design for a 2017 exhibition at Instituto Moreira Salles (IMS) São Paulo, featuring an emphasis on images and a creative use of binding. Curation: Thyago Nogueira, Valentina Tongas / Book Photos: Nino Andrés / Exhibit Photos: Pedro Vannucchi

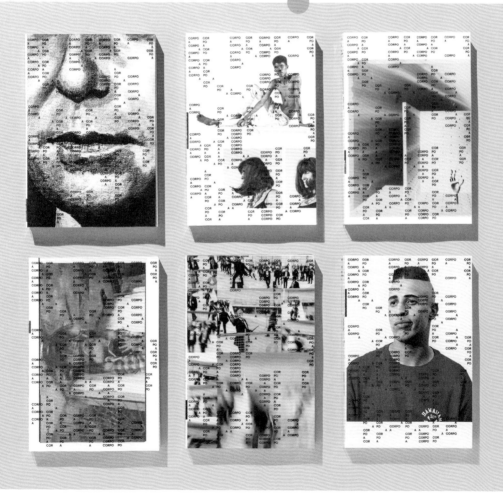

→ Linhas de Histórias
Visual identity and exhibition design for a 2017 exhibition at
Sesc Santo André featuring seven illustrators. Co-author: Flávia
Castanheira / Exhibit Photos: Nino Andrés

LINHAS DE
HISTÓRIAS

O LIVRO
ILUSTRADO
EM SETE
AUTORES

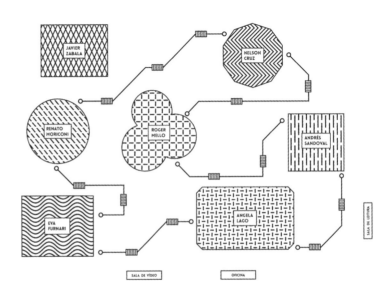

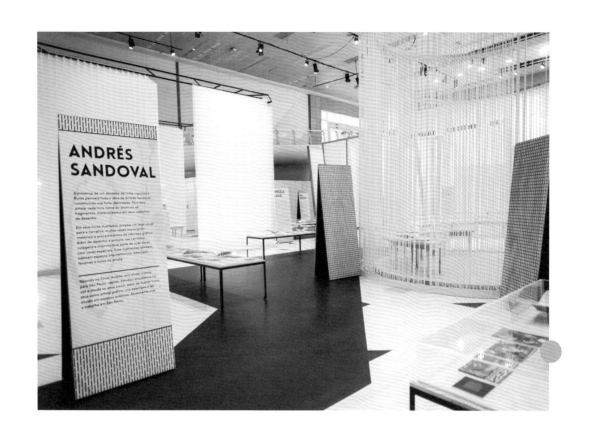

DESIGN{H}ERS

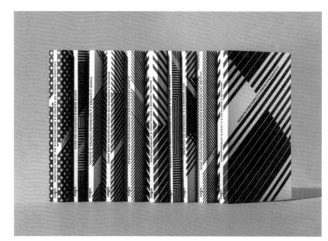

↖ Coleção Argonautas
Book design for an anthropology collection by Ubu. Graphic
Production: Lilia Goes / Book Photos: Nino Andrés

DESIGN{H}ERS

Q: What would you like to achieve through your work?

A: The main achievement of every graphic design work is communication. To reach the audience and to engage them. In times of information overload, to get real engagement is really challenging.

Q: Where do you see the future of women in design?

A: This question is too vague, so I will keep my answer as basic as possible: I hope women can reach equality in terms of professional opportunities and remuneration.

Q: How can one become more creative?

A: Creativity depends on nurturing a real interest in different things. Designers must keep themselves up-to-date on cinema, visual arts, architecture, literature, music, etc. Nowadays, we tend to get through too much superficial information, but it is increasingly difficult to establish a real connection with things, and real attention is essential for inspiration. To keep being interested and focused is hard work. For me, working in collaboration with different people with different back-grounds, designers or not, is also a source of creativity.

Q: Who are the women who inspire you?

A: It is always quite silly to drop names, but here you have a random short list: the political approach and wit of Jenny Holzer, the strength and forcefulness of Clau-dia Andujar, the beautiful flat compositions of Wanda Pimentel, the colour combinations of Eleonore Koch, the tireless search of Lygia Clark, the subtlety of Rinko Kawauchi, the wisdom of Natalia Ginzburg, etc etc etc.

Q: What do you love about being a woman?

A: To not have the pretentiousness of many men.

Q: Name the proudest moment(s) of your life.

A: This is a difficult answer... I could name some books I designed/edited, or some prizes I was lucky to win, or some very interesting people I worked with, but I don't think pride comes from specific moments. I'm proud of my work, with its highs and lows. I'm proud of my body of work, with its highs and lows. I'm proud of Ubu, the publishing house we are struggling for, day after day, with all the adversity this means in Brazil. And, I'm very proud of my kids.

Q: What brings you joy?

A: My sons, my friends, my work. Dancing, travelling abroad. Probably quite the same for everyone...

↗ Macunaíma – O Herói Sem Nenhum Caráter
Book design for a classic piece of Brazillian literature, featuring monoprints of plants and objects developed using a special technique by artist Luiz Zerbini.
Book Photos: Nino Andrés

DESIGN{H}ERS

📍 LONDON

Tina Touli

Tina Touli is a creative director, graphic communications designer, maker, speaker, and educator who currently runs her own London-based award-winning multidisciplinary studio, Tina Touli Design. Besides teaching at the world-renowned arts and design college, Central Saint Martins, she also works in a variety of design fields spanning print and digital mediums for an illustrious client list that includes Adobe, Tate, Converse, University of the Arts London, Kappa Futur Festival, and Movement Festival. She was selected by Print magazine as one of the 15 best designers in the world aged under 30 in 2017.

↓ **Movement** Festival 2018
Teaser video creation and poster
design for one of Europe's main indoor
electronic music events, in collaboration
with Smiling Sisters Production and
Kakia Konstantinaki.

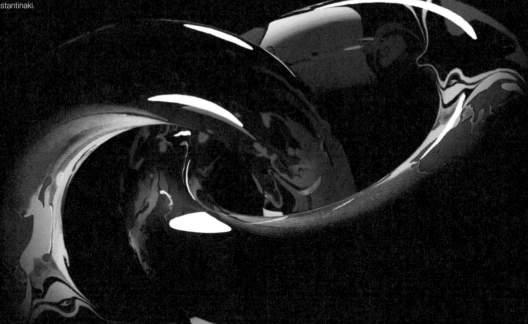

"Design is an extension of myself.
My work is my passion, and for me,
art is life and life is art."

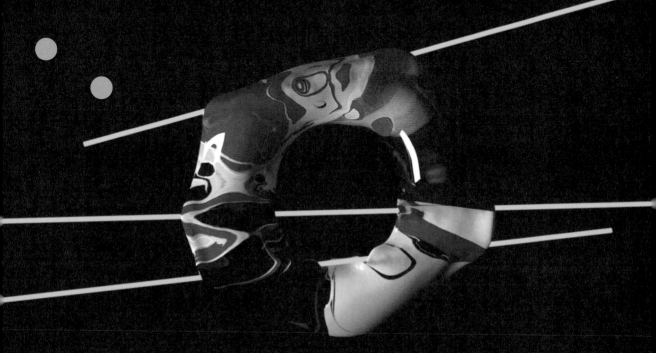

⬐ Movement Festival 2018
Teaser video creation and poster design for one of Europe's main indoor electronic music events, in collaboration with Smiling Sisters Production and Kakia Konstantinaki.

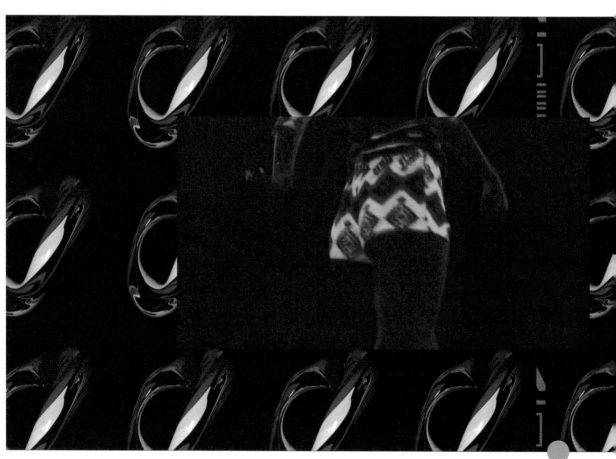

Q: What would you like to achieve through your work?

A: Design has always been my passion and is expressed through various forms of art in my everyday life, either as a simple viewer or as a creator. Every single project is a new experimentation; a new means of communication and expression. I seek inspiration from various sources, nature, technology, art, and science – always aiming to innovative and create original designs, which hopefully will inspire other creatives. It goes without saying, that the most important goal for me is to achieve the requirements of every single brief, to communicate what is supposed to be communicated, whether the messages serve social or commercial purposes.

Q: What will the future of women in design be like?

A: Women are creative, determined, passionate, and can be great leaders too. Although seeing women in leading positions is relatively recent, I believe that there are more equal opportunities nowadays. I think and really hope that in the future, we will see more women involved with design being recognised in the field and getting senior creative roles.

Q: How can one become more creative?

A: Nowadays, more and more creatives tend to follow the same processes, starting and finishing their projects on their computer, ignoring all the inspiration from our immediate surroundings. Working in front of their screen, simply reflecting without absorbing the content. Getting camouflaged into a pre-existing scene, rather than creating something new. Anything around us that can stimulate any of our senses can be inspirational and an object for investigation. A hole on a t-shirt, a wrong print, the foil paper that we wrap our food in, even the book that we read as an object itself! The more unexpected the recourse of inspiration is going to be, the more likely it is to create original work and establish your own voice. And don't forget to be passionate! Your passion is always reflected on every project's outcome. I am inclined to believe that when we fully merge ourselves with our work, we can produce the strongest outcomes.

Q: Who are the women who inspire you?

A: I have always been persistent in following my dreams and my passion for design, so any woman who does the same is an inspiration to me. I absolutely admire women who follow and accomplish their dreams, not only in work but in their everyday lives too.

Q: What do you love about being a woman?

A: The opportunity to challenge myself and prove that great design has nothing to do with someone's gender.

Q: Name the proudest moment(s) of your life

A: This is probably the hardest question for me to answer. Since my work is my passion, I would probably say that every single project I complete that had challenged me and made me feel that I can do it; overcoming any fear of failure; every recognition that I gain – no matter how small or big, are all the proudest moments of my life and what makes me happy and fulfilled.

Q: What brings you joy?

A: Design is an extension of myself. My work is my passion, and for me, art is life and life is art. Creating, challenging, and expressing myself through design as well as sharing my processes and learnings to hopefully inspire and motivate other creatives to come up with unique design solutions and find their own ways of being creative make me smile. And for as long as I am able to do that, my life will be full of joy!

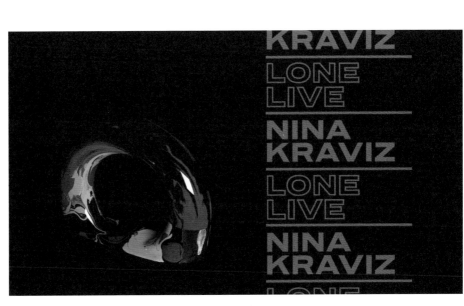

↘ 14th Athens Digital Arts Festival
Digital and print collateral design as well as teaser video creation exploring the upcoming 'technological apocalypse' under the 2018 festival theme, 'Singularity Now'. Creative Team: Jakob Ritt, Kakia Konstantinaki, Yunxin Stella Wang / Case Study Photos: Léa Abaz, Constantinos Samaras

TINA TOULI

DESIGN{H}ERS

What will you
do to tackle
the water
crisis?

22nd of
March

← 22nd of
March

What will you
do to tackle
the water
crisis?

 World
Water
Day

What will you
do to tackle
the water
crisis?

22nd of
March

WHAT
ABOUT
WATER?
WATEVER
WHO
CARES!

World
Water
Day

22nd of
March

←

What will you
do to tackle
the water
crisis?

↖ **What About Water?**
Still and moving poster design for World Water Day to question
the viewer's way of thinking towards the importance of water.
Technique Development: Jakob Ritt, Yunxin Stella Wang

Leta Sobierajski

Combining traditional graphic design elements with photography, art, and styling to create utterly unique visuals, Leta Sobierajski's work is incredibly diverse, ranging from conventional identities to brilliantly bizarre compositions. In 2016, she set up a design studio with her husband and collaborator, Wade Jeffree, through which they focus their unusual eye on projects spanning branding, art direction, installation, and videography. Besides working with an illustrious client list that includes Adobe, Google, Gucci, The New York Times, Renault, Target, and UNIQLO, Leta has also been recognised as an ADC Young Gun and continues to give talks all over the world. Her current hobbies include trimming her bangs, wearing sunscreen, and learning Japanese.

"I am proud that we are all encouraging each other to embrace self-expression and emotion."

Q: What would you like to achieve through your work?

A: I want to encourage others to know that there should not be any hesitation to add a "face" in your work. Having ownership over what you make is a feeling we should all take pride in having, and we should not be berated for making our professional work personal, especially if it comes across as an "identity". I found myself and the vernacular in which I work by using myself as the subject, because I did not have anyone else to work with. We should be able to make beautiful and impactful things with ourselves, without extravagant budgets and enormous teams.

Q: Where do you see the future of women in design?

A: The future of females will be a tolerant one. That means, females in design will be designers and not the 'token female'.

Q: How can one become more creative?

A: My favourite way to become more creative is by spending less time creating. I just turned 30, and I have spent the majority of my 20s working late nights. From 20 to 23, I spent my 9 to 5 creating unfulfilling work at a commercial job, and my evenings moonlighting to develop a personal portfolio full of meaningful work. From 24 onwards, I started a studio where even now, I struggle to turn down work because I am grateful for every opportunity and new experience, and want to make as many new things as my stamina will allow. I am too eager to work and excited to have new outlets for my ideas, but simultaneously, I need to make sure that I set aside time to enjoy sunlight, nature, and the breeze. New ideas will not come unless you give yourself time to live your life outside of design.

Q: Who are the women who inspire you?

A: The women who inspire me are typically those who exist outside of graphic design, giving me more of a perspective on living, being passionate, and valuing life and living as the most fulfilling of our goals. Perhaps this only partially counts as they are a partnership, but the work of Arakawa + Gins has been a heavy influence on my work, especially after visiting their Site of Reversible Destiny in Yoro, as well as their Reversible Destiny Lofts in Mitaka, Tokyo. Learning about the way that A + G have viewed their work as a facilitator of a 'reversible destiny' is inspiring and thought-provoking, and has caused our practice to become even more physically inclined after interacting in their spaces. I admire Madeline Gins because her relationship to her partner was so complementary and her voice was equally strong and influential. Her vision for growing younger in age by encouraging us to exercise our minds in the same way that we exercise our bodies has exponentially changed the way in which I approach my work and be involved in my practice.

Q: What do you love about being a woman?

A: I love the pride I have, and the pride that other women give me, to be confident in my mind and my body. I am proud that we are all encouraging each other to embrace self-expression and emotion.

Q: Name the proudest moment(s) of your life.

A: All of the proudest moments of my life have been those that I have been scared to pursue. I cannot pin down one in particular, but I do have a few that feel pinnacle to my development as a person and as an independently creative woman.

• Making the choice to turn my back on full-time commercial employment in order to pursue an independent, unknown career in a type of work that I found fulfilling but did not think I could find a voice in (spoiler alert: I am still constantly trying to find it).

• Allowing myself to be vulnerable enough to join an online dating platform and push through my cyber-dating stigma to have my one and only date with my now-husband and collaborative partner, Wade. I am an emotional person, but it still is not always easy for me to open up to others.

• Deciding that while work will always be fulfilling and evolving, it is still important to make choices for life experience as well as work evolution. This past summer, I decided to spend three months away from NY on my own, living in Japan and prioritising my well-being over my way of working. I plan on doing it again this summer, and as often as I can in the future.

Q: What brings you joy?

A: Travelling out of my comfort zone, eating, drinking, taking risks, and living to my fullest potential. I also love a really good glass of funky natural wine.

↖ **GUCCI Bloom**
Art direction, photography, and modelling work for a 2017 GUCCI campaign.

DESIGN{H}ERS

→ D.S. & Durga

Art direction, photography, and modelling work for a 2017 D.S. Durga campaign, in collaboration with Wade Jeffree.

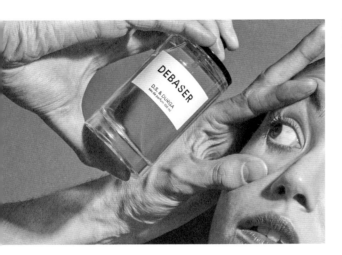

 **AIGA Eye on Design Conference**
Graphic design, art direction and prop making / styling for a 2017
conference, in collaboration with Wade Jeffree. Director: Michael
Tyburski / AIGA Eye on Design Editor-in-Chief: Perrin Drumm /
Eye Models: Wade Jeffree, Des Maher, Emma Wiseman

→ 2019 Calendar: MAKE RULES AND BREAK THEM ALL
Design focusing on type-based image creation and layer experimentation as a self-initiated project.

📍 TAIWAN / O.OO

Lu Ihwa

Founded by graphic designer Lu Ihwa, O.OO is a design studio that is dedicated to experimental work and Risograph printing solutions. Through O.OO, she believes in pushing creative boundaries with every new project by uncovering and exploring the possibilities of Risograph technology, combined with product development. From packaging design to exhibition collateral, her work has been recognised worldwide, including The Type Directors Club in New York and Tokyo.

LU IHWA @ O.OO

200

DESIGN{H}ERS

Q: What would you like to achieve through your work?

A: Every design brief that we have encountered so far has been different, so each project has brought about new learnings and inspiration. The only constant we maintain in the process of executing each project is an aptitude for experimentation, with which we try to combine various new media.

Q: Where do you see the future of women in design?

A: As a graphic designer, I have not particularly felt the difference in gender within the design industry over the past few years. As far as I am concerned, it does not matter whether the designer is a man or a woman, as the work should speak for itself. Personally, the way a designer's personality is translated through the personality of their work, is what gets my attention and a space I find very interesting.

Q: How can one become more creative?

A: Without trying to sound too profound, I think people should always pursue "their better selves". Personally, I always strive to see a different side of myself, or to look at my own limits and push myself to a new level in every creative process. As such, my tips would probably be to: be curious about yourself, and don't give up seeking to better yourself.

Q: Who are the women who inspire you?

A: I am usually most inspired by life itself, whether it is something someone suddenly said, a delicious bowl of noodles, or an earring being worn by a good friend. I like unexpected details and moments, so my inspiration cannot be tied to one specific woman.

Q: What do you love about being a woman?

A: I like it when women break the boundaries of expectations and preconceived notions! As an extreme example, many people think that one's legs should be kept 'closed' when wearing a skirt, so when a woman does the opposite, I am tickled and inspired by observing the reactions of the people around me! I think this is something that only can be done as a woman.

Q: Name the proudest moment(s) of your life.

A: Although I am not great at social activities, I participated in this year's Magical Riso Conference and tried to share my experiences, chat, and exchange ideas with other participants/speakers in a language that I am not comfortable with. I learned many things in three short days, and it was a proud moment for me.

Q: What brings you joy?

A: Life's surprising moments! Even if it is just having to get my computer fixed after it suddenly crashes, I treasure incidents like these. I lead quite a simple lifestyle, so without elements of unpredictability, my life would be "flat", or like a clean line so to speak, and I find them very enjoyable.

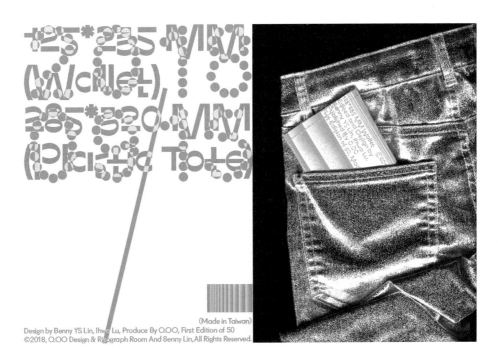

(Made in Taiwan)
Design by Benny YS Lin, Ihwa Lu, Produce By O.OO, First Edition of 50
©2018, O.OO Design & Risograph Room And Benny Lin, All Rights Reserved.

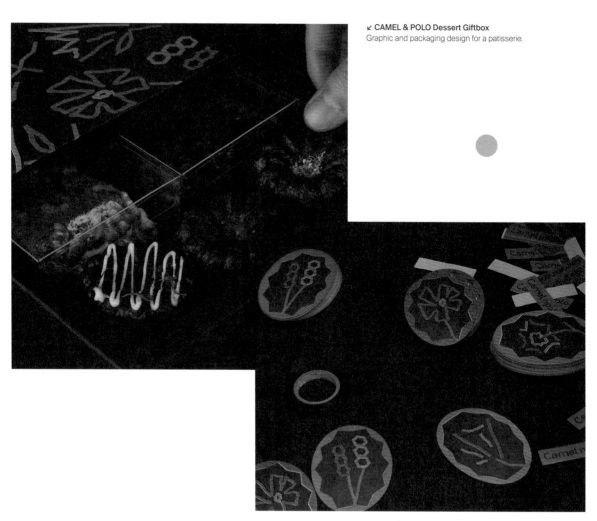

↙ **CAMEL & POLO Dessert Giftbox**
Graphic and packaging design for a patisserie.

↖ **IRMA BOOM BOOK Exhibition Visuals**
Poster and direct marketing collateral design for a 2018 exhibition featuring Irma Boom's work, organised by Not Just Library.

→ **LOVELY SUNDAY 2018**
Poster and CD design that conveys the childlike sweetness of
The Chairs' music through Risograph printing.

REAL TALK #4
THE ART OF FLOWING FEARLESSLY

↘

Hattie Stewart

justin

ANDY
WARHOL

ANDY WARHOL ARTIST ROOMS

The best is yet to come

ARTIST

HANDS OFF

SPECIAL FR

Hattie Stewart

A self-professed professional doodler who grew up in Essex, Hattie Stewart is a London-based illustrator and title designer whose work has been exhibited in Los Angeles, Miami, New York, Berlin, and London. Arguably best known for her Doodle-Bombing project, in which she has drawn over the covers of famous publications such as Interview, Vogue, i-D, and Playboy, she is also a frequent contributor to Nylon and the now-defunct Rookie magazine. Describing her work as "cheeky, playful, and a little bit dark", Hattie has collaborated with fashion-forward brands like House Of Holland, Marc By Marc Jacobs, and Adidas; and continues to delight the world at large with her bold bursts of artistic expression.

Science may have only just begun to tout the benefits of doodling as an activity that facilitates brain development, but for Hattie Stewart, it was simply a natural extension of her love of drawing from an early age. After graduating from Kingston University, she relocated to London to start her freelance career and worked hard to establish her own niche by turning doodling into a full-time gig. Fortunately, her family were very much behind her career choice. "They knew that the only thing I loved was drawing, and mama always encouraged me to make that the focus," she reveals. "They were supportive of my sister too, who was more of a designer. She is now the head of men's accessories at Loewe and the head of accessories at JW Anderson. Most of my family can draw – although not in a professional capacity – so my love for it never ceased. I was lucky that their encouragement and support helped me to thrive."

↗ **Apple Music Artwork**
Artworks featuring musicians Pharell, Adam Levine from Maroon 5, and Andra Day (page 215).

DESIGN{H}ERS

The advantages of having a strong support network are still evident in her life today in sharing her East London studio space with leading artists Lynnie Z, Sara Andreasson, and Anna Kilpelainen, who specialise in the fields of design and illustration. "Being freelancers, we all have such chaotic timetables, but when we are all together, it really is something wonderful. Our styles are so different, but there are common threads that I think work beautifully together and you can see our personalities in each one. So, even though we may not collaborate directly in our work, we do so in our support of each other and I think that is why we all get along so well and are able to flourish individually."

Although Hattie tries to make art a part of her daily programme, self employment brings with it a slew of activities that can impede creativity and the flow in general. "I actually find it quite hard to find a decent amount of time to sit down and draw. With administrative work, meetings, trying to maintain a social life, and certain pressures to keep up with a presence on social media as well as a million other things, free time for creation has to be fought for and planned in advance." While it is easy to become overwhelmed with commitments, she reflects that one's experience can shape the ways with which workload is managed. "It is all part of the freelance lifestyle that you figure out over time. I love being in the studio, and when I am there, I try to turn my phone off – which can drive some crazy, but if I do not, I just cannot get on with what I need to. If I am not drawing, I am always thinking about what I want to do next. I really have to tell myself to relax and sit back sometimes!"

Experimentation and play fuel and inform her commercial work and exhibitions, making them a crucial part of her creative process. Approaching these side projects with total freedom, her career-changing Doodle-Bomb project is the perfect example of how self-directed initiatives can take off and lead to unexpected success. "I have always been a champion of giving time to your own personal projects. I always need to be working on something that is 100% my own; if a commercial project does not go in a direction that I am proud of, at least I have created something of my own that I am. This can keep you sane, as opposed to creating through the vision of another." She is also constantly inspired by her surroundings. "I love being in London, despite the pressure such a big city can bring. There is just an endless amount of inspiring people to meet and amazing things to see."

DESIGN{H}ERS

Instead of being stifled by uncertainty, Hattie advices emerging creatives to boldly approach their side projects with purpose. "I feel that with personal projects there is no way to fail. It is all your own that you can pick up and put down whenever you need or want to. It is these explorations that will bring in the work you want to make. If it is not out there already, you can create something to fill that space and make your own little corner of the world."

While there is more than enough space for different types of artists to stand out and succeed in the scene, diversity (and the lack of it) still seems to be an issue within the creative industry. To that end, Hattie expresses her frustrations that more needs to be done to change the current situation. "It is important to make sure that diversity is also captured not only in front of the camera, but also behind it, so to speak. If I am unable to take something on, I will always do my best to make sure that I steer my clients towards those whose work would be a great fit or to shine a light on a talent whom I think is not getting the attention they rightly deserve. My fight is largely behind the scenes! I like to connect people and do my best to lift those around me, but I can always do better, as we all can."

↖ **Apple Music Artwork**
Artworks featuring musicians 5SOS and Ed Sheeran.

Hattie believes that carrying on the conversation and being open to how the conversation can change could help to tackle the issue. However, she acknowledges that it could take some time before the results are obvious. "If we keep on putting in the work to make sure that more diversity is present, by giving platforms to the voices to speak and teach and inspire, by showing and commissioning artists whose work can inspire, then I hope we will get there eventually. Change does not happen over night. It is the work put in by the generations who came before and a continuation of that labour by those that come after; it is a process."

She also thinks that industry leaders could take on a more active role in reshaping the landscape by giving precedence to creating more female spaces and hiring diverse talent. "They have to make conscious decisions to elevate the under-represented, until it subconsciously becomes part of the everyday. When we get to a point where we can say designer, instead of 'woman' designer, then we will finally be getting somewhere. At the end of the day, more diverse, creative voices make for a larger and richer industry, which can only be a good thing."

For those wishing to follow in her footsteps, Hattie is encouraging, but says that setting realistic expectations is essential, as many tend to forget how difficult it is. "It is so important not to pigeonhole yourself in the beginning into doing one thing. I was open to do doing anything to get a pay check or make a connection (within limits of course), because you never know where a job is going to come from." She also recommends a pro-active approach in getting things done, without setting expectations too high. "Get out there and meet people, but do not expect them to give you anything. Create your own personal projects based on the topics you love. Not only will it keep you sane, but it will also make you stand out and inform a lot of your commercial or paid work."

One of the most common questions she encounters is about developing a style, something which she feels is less important. She also emphasises that nothing has to be perfect, and how one's work develops is just part of the story. "Just do what you love and make a mess of it. It will just happen naturally. It cannot be forced or manipulated. Do not worry about being the best at what you do immediately. I flourished after university, many flourished a few years after, and some changed careers completely. It is all about finding out who you are and how you want to represent yourself. What I do today will not be what I do tomorrow. Enjoy the journey."

After a successful run with her commercial work, Hattie has recently decided to take some time out to pause, reflect, and refocus her energies by giving herself the space to work on her own projects. She is eager to pick up a paint brush and explore the many ideas she has been brewing, but admits that slowing down does not come easy. "I am quite hard on myself and extremely critical. I think sometimes, I forget to go slow and reflect on what I have done and the work I have made. I am always thinking of the next thing. In many ways, it has been great to be this way as it has definitely pushed me to get to where I am, but I do want to be more selective about what I want to do – it is a luxury I have worked very hard for."

The future is still a mystery, but she is not perturbed. To her, success is arbitrary in that there is no clear answer, even though she acknowledges that there needs to be the right balance of financial stability, creative fulfilment, and career recognition. "I would love to do more work in fashion and focus more on exhibiting my art – whatever allows me to keep doing what I am doing is all good by me. As long as I am able to draw everyday, make my little corner in the world, and do what I love, then I hope I will always be able to find fulfilment and happiness." Undoubtedly, an amazing corner that would be!

↑ **Postcard Design**
Illustration work in 2018.

DESIGN{H}ERS

↗ MAC Cosmetics
Artwork for MAC Cosmetics's 2016 Autumn / Winter campaign
for Paris, Shanghai, Warsaw, and Beijing.

221

"Just do what you love and make a mess of it. (Your style) will just happen naturally. It cannot be forced or manipulated."

↑ **Smiley Dots**
Personal image.

→ **Mac DeMarco**
Illustrations for the Mac DeMarco fan club.

DESIGN{H}ERS

↑ Tender Loving Care

Personal work for the Protection exhibition by Riposte Magazine and Amnesty International UK.

Morag Myerscough

Morag Myerscough's style is defined by a vibrant mix of bold colours, strong geometric or graphic patterns, and striking typography. A graduate of Central Saint Martins and the Royal College of Art, she has collaborated with renowned design agencies, public organisations, councils, and developers on meaningful projects spanning wayfinding systems, installations, and exhibitions that blur the lines between art, design, and architecture. Influenced by a variety of movements, her love for the energy and radical free expression of the 1960s continues to shape the eclectic nature of her award-winning work.

↗ **Belonging Bandstand**
Art and design work for a 2018 mobile installation
in Sussex celebrating the spirit of seminal 1960s
Los Angeles craft artist Corita Kent.

MORAG MYERSCOUGH

↑ SUPERHOT
Artwork / installation for the 7th Summer Well festival in
Bucharest, in collaboration with Luke Morgan.

DESIGN{H}ERS

Q: What would you like to achieve through your work?

A: My mantra is, 'make happy those who are near and those who are far will come' -- I want to make work that people connect to and engage and be part of. I like reactions and I don't mind if they are bad, as long as they are strong and not indifferent. Reaction and stimulation. To bring a bit of joy.

Q: Where do you see the future of women in design?

A: Stronger and stronger. I believe in equality. That is what I want to be part of achieving.

Q: How can one become more creative?

A: Believe in yourself. Have a life mission. You may not get to it immediately, but can continually reassess and if you stray, you can always get back up with the right determination. Everything does not have to be instant. Take time to think, to experience and enjoy. Work hard and be determined. Make things happen for yourself and don't think you can just depend on others to make it happen for you. Nothing comes to those who wait.

Q: Who are the women who inspire you?

A: My mother, who was an incredible person and an amazing textile artist. I have always loved the work of Bridget Riley, Barbara Kruger, and Jenny Holzer. Most recently, the incredible artist/educator and activist, Corita Kent who believed everybody could be artists. I shared an exhibition with her at Ditchling Museum of Art + Craft.

Q: What do you love about being a woman?

A: When it comes to my work, I never define myself as a women -- I feel I just do my thing. The closer we get to equality, the better it is being a woman.

Q: Name the proudest moment(s) of your life.

A: When I completed the Temple of Agape in the summer of 2015, I felt at the time that if I could never make another piece of work again, it would be okay, as I had made this one. It had so many unconscious, embedded thoughts intertwined in it. It was a release of so many deep thoughts and memories. Fortunately, I have gone on to make many more pieces of work and in 2017, I finally realised my dream of making the Belonging Bandstand. Now, I have two new personal missions coming to fruition, so hopefully, there will be a lot more proud moments to come.

The second moment was at the end of 2017, when my mother — who sadly unexpectedly died a month later — came to see me being awarded a Royal Designer for Industry. I worked so hard for my mother and father (sadly my father had died 12 years previous) to be proud of me, and I was so pleased she was there to share that moment with me.

Q: What brings you joy?

A: My partner, Luke. I feel very lucky that I found a person in this world who totally wants me to be me and embraces all my eccentricities and encourages me. When you spend so much time as I do in a super intense mind, it is so important to be able to share everyday things with another person -- especially meals. I must not forget my absolutely gorgeous 11-month old West Highland Terrier, Elvis, who is totally devoted to me and continually fills me with joy.

↖ **TEMPLE OF AGAPE**
Artwork / installation for the 2014 Festival of Love event in London, in collaboration with Luke Morgan. Photos: Gareth Gardener

↗ **SUPER LABYRINTH**
Artwork / installation for the Olympus Perspective Playground in Cologne, in collaboration with Luke Morgan.

DESIGN{H}ERS

Anna Kuts & Sevilya Nariman-qizi

Founded by Anna Kuts and Sevilya Nariman-qizi, Razöm is a design studio that also means 'together' in Ukrainian. Their work is driven by the philosophy that incredible things can only be done as an incredible team, united in thinking and interests.

Q: What would you like to achieve through your work?

A: To move away from trends by trying not to become attached to them, and instead create a product that will be unique and unusual. Unusual, sometimes incomprehensible, but very attractive. To offer the world a design product that will deal with inconvenience, visual as well as informative deformity, and at the same time, solve the tasks at-hand. To achieve maximum trust from people who collaborate with us. Trust is the most important thing, not only in design.

Q: Where do you see the future of women in design?

A: The same as the future of men in design. In today's world, occupations and opportunities are no longer determined by gender.

We think this way not because we are female, but because design is not subject to gender.

"If we talk about the future, then there are no women or men. There are design products – self-sufficient and effective – that are developed by humans."

Q: How can one become more creative?

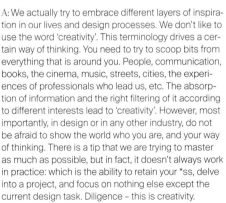

A: We actually try to embrace different layers of inspiration in our lives and design processes. We don't like to use the word 'creativity'. This terminology drives a certain way of thinking. You need to try to scoop bits from everything that is around you. People, communication, books, the cinema, music, streets, cities, the experiences of professionals who lead us, etc. The absorption of information and the right filtering of it according to different interests lead to 'creativity'. However, most importantly, in design or in any other industry, do not be afraid to show the world who you are, and your way of thinking. There is a tip that we are trying to master as much as possible, but in fact, it doesn't always work in practice: which is the ability to retain your *ss, delve into a project, and focus on nothing else except the current design task. Diligence – this is creativity.

Q: Who are the women who inspire you?

A: We can't give an exact answer to this question. There are many women from completely different spheres who are able to inspire, and singling out one of them is too difficult.

Q: What do you love about being a woman?

A: Sevilya (S) – The ability to combine grace and femininity with rigidity in decisions and actions which is usually not expected from cute creatures.

Anna (A) – Women are more impulsive and emotional beings, thanks to which they have empathic qualities. These impulses help to set the mood, whether on a sunny day, on productive work, or on a warm and cosy evening. They help in every design project that is filled with emotion, since everything is built on emotions and the reaction we seek from the viewer.

Q: Name the proudest moment(s) of your life

A: In our case, the proudest was a decision, not a moment. The decision to set aside all prejudices, fears, and unite together, organising a studio with a perspective of further growth and development in the field of design. A solution that was built on our own ambitions and future endless opportunities. Leaving the comfort zone to a position where you can't be a passive player anymore.

Q: What brings you joy?

A: (S) – Feeling in the right place at the right time. Doing the things that someone needs and thereby justifying your existence.

(A) – Balance. The balance between (doing your) favourite work and hanging out with your closest and dearest. It's great when you find the work of your life. You can completely surrender to her, but at some point, you ask yourself the question: am I happy about it? Only through the right balance and the right priorities can you maximise enjoyment from each day.

← **Takava**
Visual identity, packaging, and collateral design for a coffee-buffet / café in Kyiv. Design & Photos: Lesha Berezovskiy

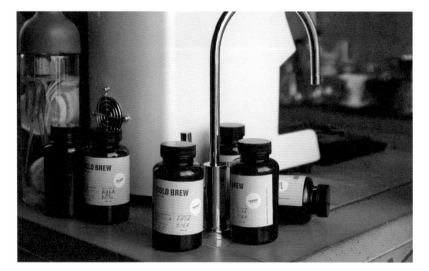

⬿ Food for the Brain
Visual identity and packaging design for a project that aims to help office workers improve their daily nutrition intake by Eat Easy food delivery service.

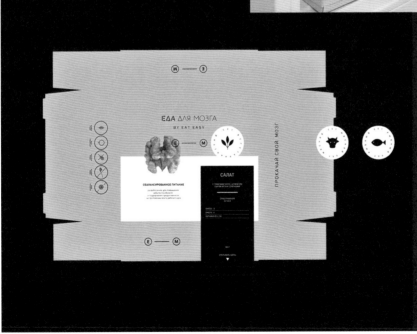

Our desire is to turn every reader into jewelry addict.

We don't teach. We advise.

Whether it is of Money, Sex or Stone are our basic topics, in which you can find related features about the jewelry world.

As far as our addiction is jewelry, our passion is people. We're here to show the way they express themselves, telling unconventional stories about simple things.

REMUSE

We want to feature you REMUSE

↙ Remuse
Visual identity development and illustration work for a media platform about the jewellery world.

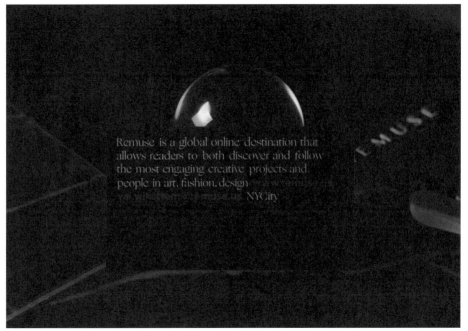

Remuse is a global online destination that allows readers to both discover and follow the most engaging creative projects and people in art, fashion, design
NYCity

↘ RAPID PROTOTYPING LANDSCAPES
Yoga mat designs as part of the RAPID PROTOTYPING
LANDSCAPES installation and performance in Berlin.

📍 LONDON / BERLIN / CROSSLUCID

Sylwana Zybura

As Creative Director and Photographer in
CROSSLUCID, an artist duo she founded with Tomas
C. Toth, Sylwana Zybura accelerates the intersections
between realities with combinations of multifaceted
visual systems and performative practices.

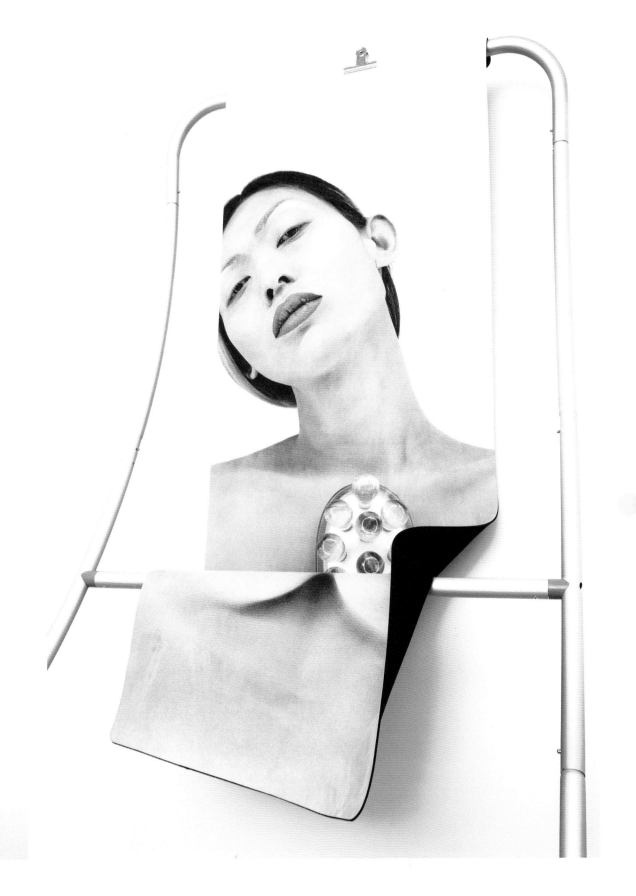

DESIGN{H}ERS

↘ **XIYANG TANG: Perception Enhancement**
Campaign work for jewellery designer, Xiyang Tang.
Model: Luke Smith / Make-up: Lauren Reynolds

SYLWANA ZYBURA @ CROSSLUCID

Q: What would you like to achieve through your work?

A: To make the recipients re-imagine the reality that they are in, give their ideas and thoughts a platform to unravel, and induce them with a sense of wonder even in everyday things and objects that do not seem enticing at first glance.

Q: Where do you see the future of women in design?

A: Hopefully, at the top of the ladder and in decision-making positions building a community and safe emotional network. Having the opportunity to develop and implement their skills without gender being an obstacle, but rather, an asset. It is not only about women, but also any non-binary professional.

Q: How can one become more creative?

A: Find a way to translate your own vision of the world that results in a unique perspective, based on your personal experiences and heritage . For me, personally, it is about open-mindedness, embracing the flow of ideas, and composing my own visually-collaged melodies. The most exciting ones to me are those so alien that I need to approach them with a child-like naiveté.

Q: Who are the women who inspire you?

A: The ones who fight, stand their ground, and not victimise themselves because of their gender.

Q: What do you love about being a woman?

A: Emotional intelligence, vulnerability, feminine power.

Q: Name the proudest moment(s) of your life.

A: All the moments I have not experienced yet.

Q: What brings you joy?

A: Creating worlds that seem impossible.

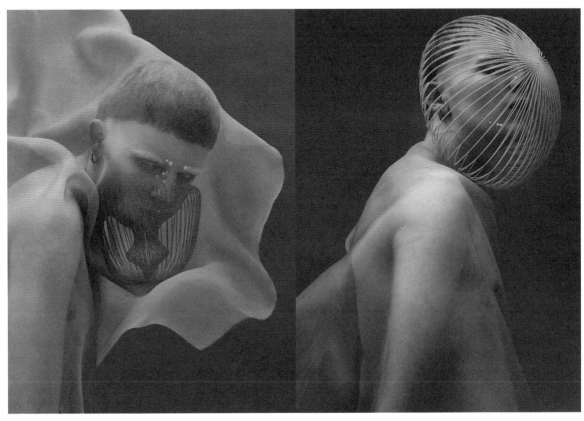

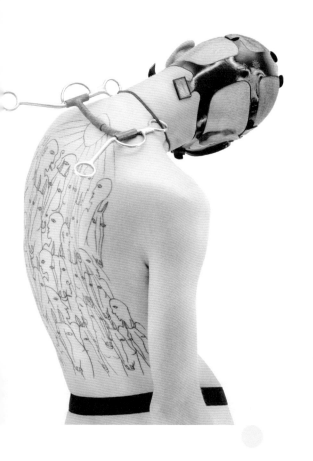

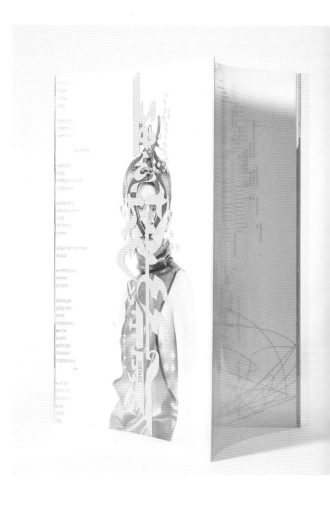

→ **LANDSCAPES BETWEEN ETERNITIES (Distanz)**
69 portraits and 28 still-life photographs documenting a two-
year long process of exploration and experimentation for a series
of multisensory exhibitions entitled '_LANDSCAPES_'.

SYLWANA ZYBURA @ CROSSLUCID

242

DESIGN{H}ERS

Jess Bonham

Texture enthusiast Jess Bonham's playful imagery stems from her love of pattern, precision, reinvention and curious correlations. Besides mixing luxurious textures with unexpected objects to find a new form of beauty through narratives, intrigue, and bold juxtapositions, she also embraces the translation of sculptural objects into photographs and moving images – often with the injection of humour and surprise. After studying illustration at Brighton University where she focused her enthusiasm for composition and photography within mixed media collages, Jess developed and adapted her technique to eventually work entirely within the camera.

Q: What would you like to achieve through your work?

A: Eye-catching, thought-provoking imagery that makes people smile.

Q: Where do you see the future of women in design?

A: I think women will continue to make amazing work alongside, and equal to, their male contemporaries.

Q: How can one become more creative?

A: Go on adventures away from the internet and let yourself be guided by your own intuition in response to the world around you.

Q: Who are the women who inspire you?

A: Grace Jones, Vivienne Westwood, Sally Mann, Zadie Smith, Anna Lomax, my mum... to name but a few.

Q: What do you love about being a woman?

A: I love the bond of female friendships. Sisterships are key to a happy and balanced mindset, so I feel very lucky to be a woman in that regard.

Q: Name the proudest moment(s) of your life.

A: Giving birth to my daughter.

Q: What brings you joy?

A: My daughter, walking outdoors with my dog, mouth-watering colour pairings, a good brief, fresh nails!

↖ Visual Noise
Work for a 2016 exhibition, where the imagery was designed to represent the quality of specific sounds. Set Design: Anna Lomax / Curation: Studio Small, East Photographic

DESIGN{H}ERS

JESS BONHAM   246

↙ Google Meet
Photography and wallpaper UI design for a video-conferencing
application by Google Hangouts. Set Design: Anna Lomax

↘ Domestic Assembly
Photography for a 2017 project that explored the process of collecting
furniture design pieces for the home (including page 248). Set Design:
Natalie Turnball / Furniture: Augustus Greaves

DESIGN{H}ERS

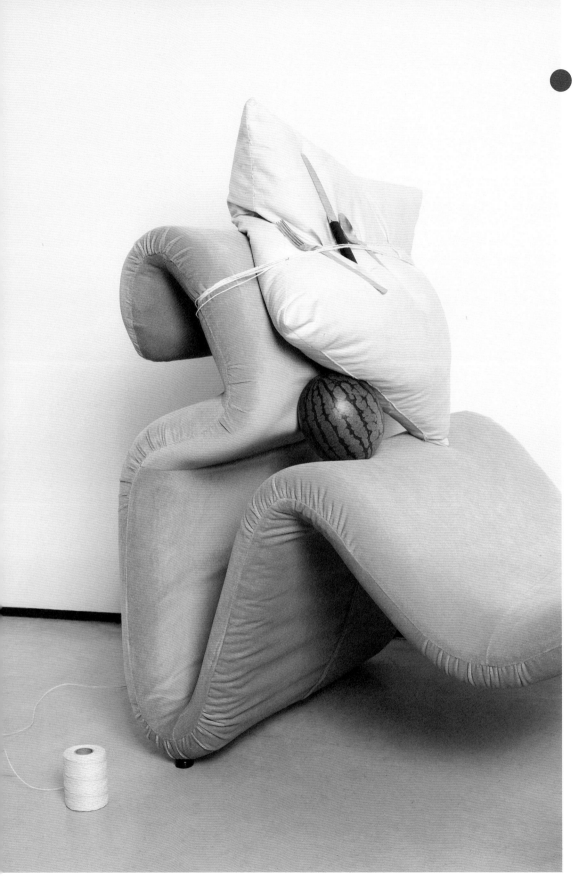

DESIGN{H}ERS

"I love the bond of female friendships. Sisterships are key to a happy and balanced mindset."

↗ Wonderland
Work for Wonderland magazine's Outspoken issue, in collaboration with Anna Lomax.

JESS BONHAM

DESIGN{H}ERS

 BARCELONA

Birgit Palma

Originally from Austria, Birgit Palma is a multidisciplinary illustrator and lettering addict who is passionate about deepening her love for illustration. She is partial to bold designs, op art, as well as abstract and colourful geometry. After completing her studies in Salzburg and becoming an art director in several studios around the world, Birgit founded her own studio in Barcelona to find the sweet spot between modern illustration and avant-garde design. She continues to work with a wide range of international clients in the advertising, fashion, and editorial industries.

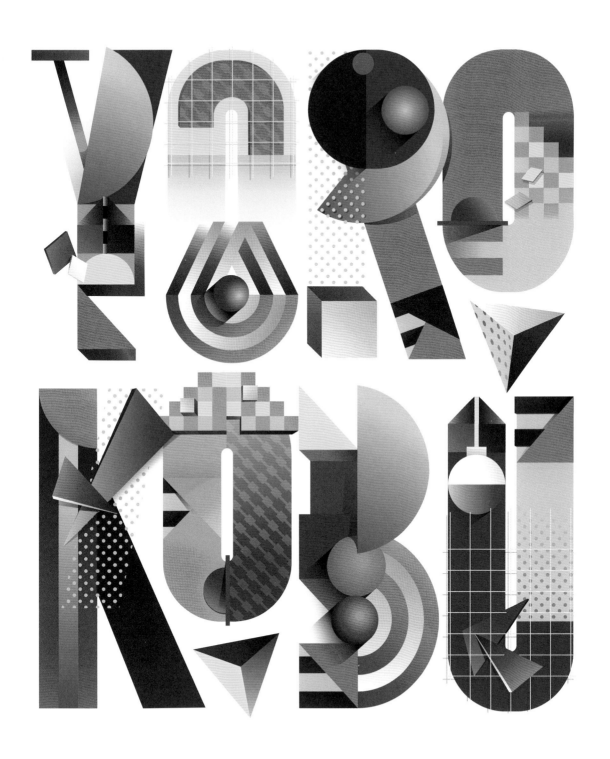

↑ **YOROKOBU #91: Cover Illustration**
Illustrated type for Yorokobu magazine's January 2017 issue cover.

DESIGN{H}ERS

Q: What would you like to achieve through your work?

A: My artworks are positive, bold, talkative – they are fun. The world is so d*mned busy and serious nowadays, so I want people to pause for a moment, take in the beauty of art, and smile. I want them to enjoy what they see, and also maybe decipher the underlying message. Vision is a powerful tool; able to influence how we feel and behave.

Q: Where do you see the future of women in design?

A: Everywhere. I don't see any area of design where women can't achieve the same thing as men. Designers shouldn't define themselves by their gender or let others define them. In the end, it should be the work that gets paid with respect.

Q: How can one become more creative?

A: Slow down. Get away from the computer. Breathe in the world by immersing yourself in all the hustle and bustle, then get inspired by everything around you – whether it is design, nature, or even just a good chat with Grandma.

Q: Who are the women who inspire you?

A: Tricky question! I am inspired by every single mother on earth. Special admiration goes out to all mothers who manage to combine their professional lives with the birth of a child. High fives to Marta Cerda, Jessica Hische, Paula Scher, and countless others who manage both successfully. I was also deeply impressed by Pentagram partner Marina Willer's lecture, which talked about how private 'things' like family influence her in her work.

Q: What do you love about being a woman?

A: One of the most interesting things about being a woman is experiencing the changes of your body over a lifetime. Men will never be able to feel their boobs grow or have a new life inside them – take that!

Q: Name the proudest moment(s) of your life.

A: That's a tough one. I've actually never thought about it. Maybe my proudest moment can't be traced to a certain point. I guess it's the awareness that I can do it all by myself (which means that I can survive on my own). I also teach in the University of Applied Sciences in Salzburg and am always proud to see the creative development of my students, especially if I can help them.

Q: What brings you joy?

A: Life itself. Simple things like having a beer with friends, going hiking, breathing in the smell of the ocean or leaving work a couple of hours earlier, and it's Friday :-)

↘ **Oxymora**
Display font design inspired by M.C. Escher's optical
illusions as a self-initiated project in 2016.

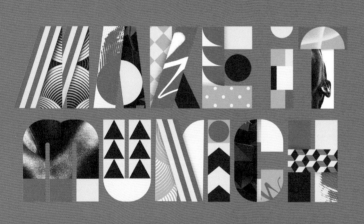

Made with Love & Adobe Creative Cloud & Adobe Stock

Made with Love & Adobe Creative Cloud & Adobe Stock

↖ Adobe Make It: Modular Lettering Workshop
Design development in collaboration with Daniel Triendl for a series of workshops in 2017 about creating typography using modular raster as a preset, held by Adobe Germany and Faktor 3.

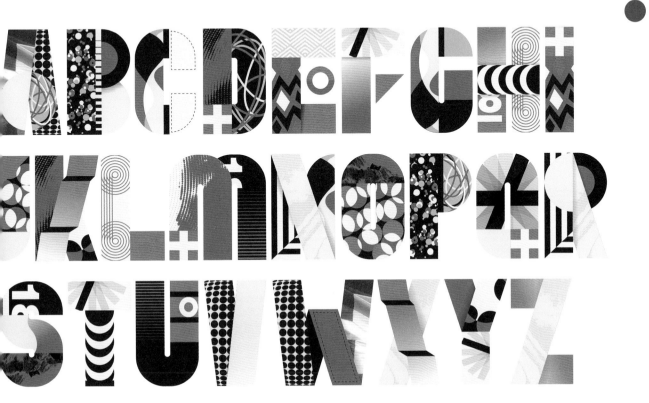

Asuka Watanabe

Graphic designer, illustrator, and art director Asuka Watanabe expresses herself through geometric, colourful visuals as well as simple themes to create unique outcomes across mediums, spanning logo and UI design to painting. She finds inspiration in all areas of life to deliver a combination of fine art and industrial design work.

Q: **What would you like to achieve through your work?**

A: I would be happy if our lives became more brilliant and fun with my design/art.

Q: **Where do you see the future of women in design?**

A: Expressions will become more diverse, and designs will become more unique.

Q: **How can one become more creative?**

A: One of the most important things is simply to keep being inspired by anything. I would go to exhibitions, or out into the countryside to get inspiration. This way, I gradually developed my own style. So, my advice would be to keep designing and being inspired by anything around you.

Q: **Who are the women who inspire you?**

A: Yayoi Kusama! Her art is so powerful and unique.

Q: **What do you love about being a woman?**

A: Being a woman is part of my own originality. I love making 'kawaii' and feminine things.

Q: **Name the proudest moment(s) of your life.**

A: When I was a band in high school, I was in charge of making posters and flyers. It was fun, and my band-mates loved my work. From there, I was inspired to go further into design.

Q: **What brings you joy?**

A: I want to continue creating what I love, and it would be great if someone likes my design.

DESIGN{H}ERS

↘ FUJI ROCK FESTIVAL 2017
Visual art and graphic design for an annual music
festival organised by Smash.

DESIGN{H}ERS

→ Rosee
Visual identity design for a hair salon in Tokyo. Architecture:
Arashiro Hiroaki (aadpool) / Design Assistance & French
Translation: Pauline Guerini / Photos: Haruyuki Shirai

DESIGN{H}ERS

ASUKA WATANABE

INDEX

{

"Being a woman is part of my own originality. I love making 'kawaii' and feminine things."

Asuka Watanabe

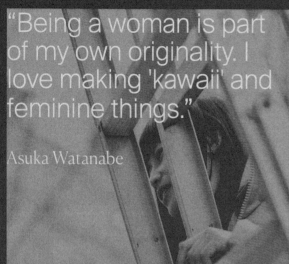

"I think being a woman gives me a different viewpoint and approach to work and life."

Beci Orpin

"I often try and imagine how I used to feel when I was a child when approaching projects. I want unadulterated happiness."

Camille Walala

Carolina Cantante & Catarina Carreiras / Studio AH—HA
↗ studioahha.com
↗ P. 025-031

Camille Walala
↗ camillewalala.com
↗ P. 128-135

Charry Jeon / CFC
↗ contentformcontext.com
↗ P. 040-045

Elaine Ramos / UBU
↗ elaineramos-estudiografico.com.br
↗ P. 176-183

"Never look at other designers for inspiration. Instead, be as 'you' as you can be. This is where your creaative joy and point of difference are most in sync."

Eva Dijkstra

Eva Dijkstra
/ Design by Toko
↗ designbytoko.com
↗ P. 058-063

"I think one of the main things I love about being a woman is feeling like I have both the ability (and permission) to really work to understand myself from the inside out."

Jessica Hische

"New ideas will not come unless you give yourself time to live your life outside of design."

Leta Sobierajski

Leslie David
↗ leslie-david.com
↗ P. 136-142

Lotta Nieminen
↗ lottanieminen.com
↗ P. 089-097

"I love the movement that has been going on lately. Women are speaking up and it feels amazing to be taken seriously more often."

Louise Mertens

Louise Mertens
↗ louisemertens.com
↗ P. 032-039

Lu Ihwa / O.OO
↗ odotoo.com
↗ P. 200-206

"Be curious about yourself, and don't give up seeking to better yourself."

Lu Ihwa

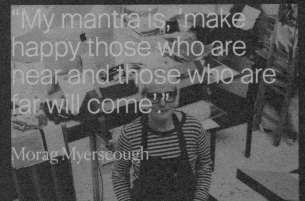

"My mantra is, 'make happy those who are near and those who are far will come'."

Morag Myerscough

Morag Myerscough
↗ studiomyerscough.com
↗ P. 225-231

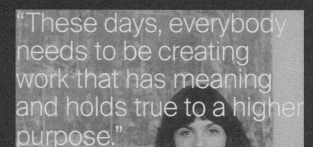

"These days, everybody needs to be creating work that has meaning and holds true to a higher purpose."

Roanne Adams

"Building relationships and trust, as well as listening and having patience, maintaining a good sense of diplomacy, and multitasking are all skills that come naturally to many women."

Susanna Nygren Barrett

Tina Touli
↗ tinatouli.com
↗ P. 184-191

Verònica Fuerte / Hey
↗ heystudio.es
↗ P. 073-088

"A studio takes a lot of effort; not only in designing, but also in investing in the people you work with as well as the clients. Nobody teaches you how to run a studio or manage people. I made a lot of mistakes in the beginning, but you learn from them."

Verònica Fuerte

Yu Yah-Leng / Foreign Policy Design Group
↗ foreignpolicy.design
↗ P. 143-158

Yu Qiongjie / Tran-swhite Studio
↗ transwhite.cn
↗ P. 046-051

"Inspiration is a continuous movement, not a special occasion."

Vanessa Eckstein

Vanessa Eckstein / Blok Design
↗ blokdesign.com
↗ P. 168-175

↘ ACKNOWLEDGEMENTS
We would like to thank all the designers, studios, and companies who participated in the production of this book for their significant contributions to its compilation. We would also like to express our gratitude to all the producers involved for their invaluable opinions and assistance, as well as the professionals in the creative industry who were generous with their insights and feedback throughout the entire production process. Last but not least, to those who made specific input behind the scenes but were not credited within these pages, we appreciate all your efforts and continuous support.

↘ FUTURE EDITIONS
If you wish to participate in viction:ary's future projects and publications, please send your website address or portfolio to submit@victionary.com